"Effective change management is one of the most essential skills for any leader – this book is a great reader for those new to leadership and those who need an insightful refresher. It's accessible with real and relevant examples and based clearly on the broad experience of the authors and the individuals and organisations they've worked with. It's the sort of book you'll pick up for one purpose and then find that you're drawn into – wanting (and needing) to read more and more."
—**Iain Watson,** *Director, Tyne & Wear Archives & Museums*

"*Managing Change in Museums and Galleries* inspires, educates and empowers the reader to approach change in their museum with confidence. It is the book that I wish I'd had to support me over the last 25 years of my museum career. It applies concepts and theory to real life challenges, drawing on strong case studies from in and outside the museum sector. It is an invaluable guide to navigating change, and the challenges and opportunities it brings, in museums today."
—**Emma Chaplin,** *Director, Association of Independent Museums*

MANAGING CHANGE IN MUSEUMS AND GALLERIES

Managing Change in Museums and Galleries is the first practical book to provide guidance on how to deal with organisational change in museums, galleries or heritage organisations.

Written by two authors who have direct experience of leading change, running change programmes and advising on change in more than 250 museums and galleries, the book identifies the various problems, issues and challenges that any professional in a museum or heritage organisation is likely to encounter and provides advice on how to deal with them. The book's six parts treat change holistically, and help the reader understand what change entails, prepare for it and lead it, ensure that everyone in the museum is involved, understand what can go wrong and evaluate and learn from it. Each chapter is devoted to a specific challenge that is often encountered during change and is extensively cross-referenced to other relevant chapters. Including a list of helpful resources and suggestions of useful publications for further reading, this book is a unique guide to change in museums.

Managing Change in Museums and Galleries is an essential resource for all museum practitioners – whether they be the people in museums and galleries who are leading change, or those affected by change as a leader, a member of staff or a volunteer.

Piotr Bienkowski has over 35 years of experience in the museum, arts, heritage and culture sector. As Director of the *Our Museum* programme, he oversaw one of the most extensive programmes of organisational change in the sector in recent times, working with nine museums across the UK to embed community engagement in their organisations. He has also been Deputy and Acting Director of Manchester Museum, and Professor of Archaeology and Museology at the University of Manchester, and he now advises a wide range of museums, galleries and heritage organisations as a consultant.

Hilary McGowan works with museums, galleries and heritage organisations to help them change, so they can thrive in the future. Her distinguished track record includes successfully leading major museums through change in York, Exeter and Bristol, increasing visitor numbers and boosting income. Hilary established her own business 25 years ago and has worked with over 200 different museums throughout the UK. As the principal museum Trustee at Bletchley Park for ten years, she played a leading role in the transformation of the Museum from mere survival to curatorial and commercial prosperity.

Routledge Guides to Practice in Museums, Galleries and Heritage

This series provides essential practical guides for those working in museums, galleries, and a variety of other heritage professions around the globe.

Including authored and edited volumes, the series will help to enhance practitioners' and students' professional knowledge and will also encourage sharing of best practices between different countries, as well as between different types and sizes of organisations.

Titles include:

Interpreting Heritage
A Guide to Planning and Practice
Steve Slack

Managing Change in Museums and Galleries
A Practical Guide
Piotr Bienkowski and Hilary McGowan

For more information about this series, please visit: www.routledge.com/Routledge-Guides-to-Practice-in-Museums-Galleries-and-Heritage/book-series/RGPMGH

MANAGING CHANGE IN MUSEUMS AND GALLERIES

A Practical Guide

Piotr Bienkowski and Hilary McGowan

Routledge
Taylor & Francis Group

LONDON AND NEW YORK

First published 2021
by Routledge
2 Park Square, Milton Park, Abingdon, Oxon OX14 4RN

and by Routledge
52 Vanderbilt Avenue, New York, NY 10017

Routledge is an imprint of the Taylor & Francis Group, an informa business

British Library Cataloguing-in-Publication Data
A catalogue record for this book is available from the British Library

Library of Congress Cataloging-in-Publication Data
A catalog record for this book has been requested

ISBN: 978-0-367-85851-3 (hbk)
ISBN: 978-0-367-85850-6 (pbk)
ISBN: 978-1-003-01539-0 (ebk)

Typeset in Bembo
by Apex CoVantage, LLC

CONTENTS

FIGURES

TABLES

ACKNOWLEDGEMENTS

The authors would like to thank the many colleagues who have helped with this book – the ones specifically mentioned below, as well as the hundreds of colleagues and clients we have worked with over many years with whom we garnered the experience and reflection that is shared in these pages.

Many thanks to:

Emma Chaplin, Association of Independent Museums; Iain Watson, Tyne & Wear Museums & Archives; and Sharon Heal, Museums Association, for support and endorsements.

Maggie Appleton, RAF Museum and President of the Museums Association; Jeff Cowton, Cumbria Museums Consortium; Mary Godwin, Bodmin Keep Army Museum; Emmie Kell, Cornwall Museums Partnership; Anna Brennand, formerly Ironbridge Gorge Museums Trust; Tamsin Russell, Museums Association; and Diana Zeuner, for interviews and thought-provoking discussion.

Nina Simon for her inspiring Foreword, as well as ideas, encouragement and references both before and during the writing of the book.

Nuala Morse, Department of Museum Studies, University of Leicester, for discussions and suggestions when this book was just an idea.

The anonymous reviewers of the original book proposal, who made helpful pointers to aspects we had missed.

Heidi Lowther and Katie Wakelin at Routledge, who have been super-helpful and easy to work with, always prompt and clear with their responses to any queries.

Hilary thanks her husband, Grant, for his hugs and encouragement during lockdown in 2020.

FOREWORD

In June 2020, the nonprofit organisation OF/BY/FOR ALL ran a poll on one very simple question:

If a trusted funder offered your organisation a blank cheque right now for one of the following paths forward, what would you do with the money?

A   Use it to pay our team and come back to normal operation (with healthy reserves!) when it is safe to do so.
B   Use it as risk capital to pay our team to radically reinvent our programmes, services and business model.
C   Redirect the money to other organisations and people who are in greatest crisis right now.
D   Let the existing organisation die and use the money to build something totally new.

Across 1,000 respondents from cultural institutions around the world, 57 per cent opted for B – to take the risk and reinvent everything. If you're picking up this book, my guess is you are among this 57 per cent. You see the potential for change at your organisation. You see the potential to become more relevant and valued in your community. You see glaring issues to fix, systems to break and rebuild and new goals to pursue.

That's wonderful. That's the way I see museums, too.

But I invite you – for a moment – to consider your colleagues who did not pick option B. The people who, despite the enormity of what the world demands of us, do not feel called to change. The preservationists who would prefer to hunker down and wait for the clouds to part. The professionals who see change as inappropriate or poor form. The cynics who have been burned in previous attempts to make change. The meek who are hesitant to try.

There are many such people in our organisations. When I started out as a young changemaking museum director, I naively saw these people as enemies. I assumed they were fundamentally disagreeable, prejudiced or opposed to change. I drew battle lines between 'us', who wanted to build an inclusive future, and 'them', who wanted to protect an elitist relic.

I quickly learned how short-sighted I was and how poorly this perspective would serve me. I learned most people don't fear change. They fear loss. They fear grief. They fear having their hearts broken because something close to them has moved far away. And because of this fear, they are not equipped for change. They don't see the future in it – or often, they don't imagine a role for themselves in that future.

To lead change, I learned to invite people into that possible future. I learned to make my intentions clear and inviting. I learned to ask people to consider that loss might come with gain. I learned to stop thinking about 'us' and 'them' and instead to think about how I could invite people who were invested in the past to write themselves into a different future. Instead of casting people out, I asked them to choose to pitch in.

To me, choice is the crux of institutional change. It's not about whether you need to change or want to change. It's not about whether you fear it or hunger for it. It's about whether you choose to change.

Change is hard. But choosing to change – that should feel easy. Change is a choice you make every day when you get up in the morning. It's a choice you can hold yourself and others accountable to. The choice is a gift that propels you through the hard stuff, the change you want and the change you don't.

This, to me, is why this book is not called 'making' change but 'managing' change. When you manage change, you don't just plough through and do what you like. You don't give up when it doesn't work out. You choose to launch a change process. You invite others in. You explain why it matters. You paint a picture of a beguiling destination, and you encourage people to sketch themselves into that future. You listen calmly as people shake their fists and shout that your change is going to ruin everything. You accept praise and redirect it to your team, or use it to build momentum for a hard choice ahead. You show up with energy and hope each day, and you watch as the change spreads, from your own heart to the hearts of your colleagues, community partners and stakeholders.

Of course, it all sounds lovely in the abstract. But it's damn hard work. I know what it's like first hand. In 2011, at the age of 29, I became the director of a small museum in California that was on the brink of closure. I didn't know much about the organisation, but they had a vision statement to become a 'thriving central gathering place'. I knew this vision was only possible if we changed deeply – and fast.

My first week on the job, I asked staff to join me in taking a 20 per cent salary cut. I told my new colleagues I believed our organisation could and should have a bigger impact – and that we could do it if we worked in deep partnership with our diverse community. I asked them to work with me to try to build that museum. And while some of these people were no doubt sceptical, stressed, scared, or confused, they chose to get involved. They chose to work together to change.

My playbook for change mirrors much of what you'll read in this book. It was driven by an intense external stimulus – a lack of funds and relevance. We used that impetus to develop a strong vision. We brought in many new voices as staff, trustees, partners and volunteers. We experimented – imperfectly. We celebrated together when the vision became real in the form of new visitors, programmes, energy, funding and meaning.

We often got it wrong. Sometimes I got hurt, and sometimes I hurt others. Institutional change involves a breaking and remaking that can be confusing, upsetting and painful. I grew accustomed to the phenomenon of the 'good/bad' meeting, where it was good because it had gone badly. I took angry phone calls from disillusioned former supporters. I learned to treat detractors with compassion, even as I stayed focused on the path we'd chosen to change. And I tried to protect my team – and myself – when the vision got demeaned, distorted and thrown back in my face.

Over time, more and more of us chose to change. We chose, together, to build a more inclusive, relevant institution. We managed change like one might manage a garden, planting seeds, encouraging volunteers, clearing weeds, cleaning up after storms, watering, feeding, pruning and cultivating the work towards the vision.

Like a garden, the change I led was not permanent. Nor likely will yours be. The museum kept shifting during my eight years as director, and, after I left, it continued to shift further. Today, I watch my former museum keep changing from the sidelines. Sometimes I cheer. Sometimes I mourn. But every day I know the choice to change was worth it.

Nina Simon

Nina Simon is Founder and CEO, OF/BY/FOR ALL, and author of *The Art of Relevance* and *The Participatory Museum*.

INTRODUCTION

The challenge of change

Organisational change is one of the biggest challenges facing museums and galleries across the world today.[1] The need to change is usually a response to different external pressures. Often these are financial deficits, demands that museums and galleries alter their missions and business models to address funding priorities more directly or the ability of museums to be more responsive to the public and engage with diverse and marginalised audiences. Globally, financial pressures have built up in recent years. There has been a general trend to extract better value for money in public services, and this will certainly continue for the foreseeable future given the state of the global economy.

On occasion, of course, external change agents – not all man-made – have caused wider disruption, and have impacted a larger number of museums, such as terrorism; the AIDS, Ebola and SARS epidemics; or flooding and other weather disruptions, but these have usually been limited geographically or socially. It so happens that this book is being published in the wake of the most devastating and wide-ranging of these, the 2020 Covid-19 pandemic. This was a disaster for museums and galleries across the whole world, most of which had to close for many months, losing income and shedding staff. The impact will be felt for many years, and the need for change to respond to this sudden and unexpected crisis is affecting every single organisation, in terms of finance, staffing and finding a role to serve their communities.

Few were immune from the need for change even in normal times. Some of this change was imposed, for example when funders and stakeholders bailed a museum or gallery out of financial crisis, and some of it was voluntary, as when a governing body recognised the need for change and proactively responded to external pressure from stakeholders or communities or a lack of funding. Organisational change often involves financial cuts and 'efficiency savings', and can include changes to aims and mission, staff restructures, role changes and redundancies and fundamental shifts in fundraising and commercial activities. Potentially, it can affect everyone working in a museum or gallery. In the wake of the pandemic, all of these factors are true for all museums and galleries across the world – response to a pandemic is little different from a response to any other major crisis, but it affects everyone at the same time and as a result the usual sources of external support are overstretched. The need for change is no longer an option – it is essential.

Yet, despite change having been a common fact of museum and gallery life for decades, in the authors' experience much change fails to achieve its goals or seems to take so long that everyone involved loses focus (and patience). Staff faced with the introduction of a change programme often automatically equate it with restructuring and redundancies; as a result, fear for their jobs sets up a resistance which can undermine the whole change programme. Across all sectors, including culture, it is widely reported that at least 70 per cent of attempts at organisational change fail, and those that succeed do so only after about five years.[2] There are common factors behind the failure of change initiatives, and common strands in their success. The purpose of this book is to bring those out in a practical, accessible way that will allow your change programme to succeed, adapt and be sustainable. Having a workable plan for change is more important now than ever before.

The guidance and learning in this book are applicable to all types of museums around the world, and we have incorporated examples and case studies from a range of countries with different museum environments. The existing literature on long-term change in the museum sector is sparse. There are only three case studies worldwide in which long-term change, over many years, has been carried out, recorded, analysed and the transferable learning drawn out and published. Two of these are on individual museums – Robert Janes on Glenbow Museum in Canada, and Nina Simon on Santa Cruz Museum in California – while one is on a long-term programme of change across nine museums and galleries in the UK (the *Our Museum* programme, directed by one of the authors). Useful lessons on change are also found in the publications of the UK *Circuit* programme and, in the USA, the James Irvine Foundation's New California Arts Fund evaluation. Outside the museum sector, the study of change at the Royal Shakespeare Company also has relevant and valuable lessons for museums and galleries.[3]

This book is based on the authors' direct experiences of leading change, running change programmes, advising on change and being part of change in more than 250 museums and galleries, mostly in the UK but also in Europe. These range from the smallest volunteer-run museums to the largest multi-site organisations, cover all forms of governance (independent, local authority, university, regimental and national museums) and all types of collections (art, archaeology, ethnography, science, local history, rural and industrial museums).

The structure of this book and how to use it

This book is about managing and dealing with change. It is explicitly aimed at practitioners – the people in museums and galleries who are leading change or are affected by change. It is about the practicalities of change: a guide to all the challenges you are likely to encounter during change and how to deal with them, whether as a leader, a staff member or a volunteer affected by change.

The book is divided into six parts. These are arranged logically from defining change, to preparing for it, leading it, dealing with it as a staff member or volunteer, understanding why change fails and evaluating and learning from it:

Part 1: What Is Change?
Part 2: Preparing for Change
Part 3: Leading Change
Part 4: The Role of Staff and Volunteers in Change
Part 5: Why Change Fails
Part 6: Evaluating and Learning from Change

The book comprises 56 chapters divided among these six parts. Each chapter is devoted to a specific topic that you might encounter on your change journey, for example, 'What makes a good change leader?', or 'Countering resistance to change'. At the end there are lists of *Resources to Help You* (primarily a list of practically focused web-based resources on change in museums and galleries) and *Useful Publications* – these are, deliberately, not an exhaustive list of literature on change in museums (much of which is theoretical and/or aimed at academics), but strictly books and papers that practitioners might find useful when dealing with change on the ground.

Spoiler alert! This is not a 'how-to' guide or a toolkit, because organisational change is not linear and will be different in every museum or gallery. We do not wish to mislead readers that they can follow this book, step by step, as a toolkit for change. Instead, the book identifies all the various considerations, problems and challenges that any museum's change process is likely to encounter and gives practical advice on how to deal with each one. Of course, these are often interlinked, and so each theme-based chapter is cross-referenced to other relevant chapters.

Earlier, we noted the scarcity of case studies on long-term change. The learning from these has been incorporated into this book and the case studies are cited where appropriate. There are also case studies from the authors' own experiences of change management, but for reasons of confidentiality these have usually been anonymised. However, accounts of case studies have been kept to a minimum. The purpose of this book is to offer concise and practical guidance, not detailed case studies, which in any event can occasionally date quickly, or are perceived (rightly or wrongly) as not relevant to a particular museum or type of museum. For that reason, in most chapters our preferred approach has been to use quotations from practitioners, which reveal their responses and insights regarding particular approaches to change. In other work, we have found that readers respond positively to these sorts of short quotations rather than lengthy and perhaps less immediately relevant case studies.

One of the basic principles of the authors' approach – borne out time and again in their work over many years – is that for change to be successful it must involve everyone and be everyone's responsibility, not just that of directors and boards. This is a thread that runs through the book. As a result, this book is aimed at all practitioners involved in change: directors, managers, governing bodies, staff members, volunteers and strategic partners. There are always actions that anyone can take – whatever their role – to help shape and deal with change. Everyone has the capacity, and the responsibility, to be a change agent.

We envisage that the typical practitioner-user, in search of practical and concise guidance, will start by consulting a particular chapter whose topic they are encountering in their museum/gallery, and will then find cross-references to other related chapters – thus using the book in the manner of a trouble-shooting guide, rather than something to be read systematically from cover to cover. Nevertheless, the sequencing of the six parts of the book also encourages practitioners (especially leaders) to think holistically about change – to understand what it entails, to prepare for it, involve everyone, implement it successfully, be aware of what can go wrong and evaluate and learn from the process.

For convenience and to avoid unnecessary duplication, throughout the book the word 'museum' should be understood to include both museums and art galleries. The guidance is also transferable to other cultural organisations. The authors have found that archives, heritage sites, libraries, and science and discovery centres have similar challenges to museums, and that the same approaches to managing change are also effective there.

Notes

1 For the challenges facing museums and their need to change, see, for example, G. Black, *Transforming museums in the twenty-first century* (Routledge 2012), pp. 1–6 and *Museums and the challenge of change: Old institutions in a new world* (Routledge 2021).
2 R. Hewison, J. Holden and S. Jones, *All together: A creative approach to organisational change* (Demos 2010), p. 19.
3 Full references to these case studies are in Chapter 53 and the *Resources to Help You* and *Useful Publications* sections at the end of the book.

PART 1

What is change?

It is often taken for granted that everyone in museums and galleries understands what 'change' is, but, in practice, this is not necessarily the case. Part 1 defines the nature of change, and what it is that museums and galleries are actually changing, so that everyone involved and affected can understand up front what change may entail, be prepared for it and take an active part in it.

It describes and explains the common factors of all successful change programmes: they take time; the strategic vision needs to be long term as museums need to be long-term organisations; small changes in many different areas, across the whole museum, add up to significant transformation; and change is everyone's responsibility and job – not only leaders and governing bodies but all staff and volunteers can become change agents.

As noted in the Introduction, throughout this book the word 'museum' will refer to both museums and art galleries.

1

WHAT ARE YOU CHANGING?

> The future of successful museums will be one of constant repositioning to adapt to, or outwit, the forces of change.
> Michael Ames, University of British Columbia Museum of Anthropology[1]

When museums talk about 'organisational change', exactly what is it that they are proposing to change? For many staff, 'change' is perceived as shorthand for redundancies, and this can immediately set up a resistance to the process.

As reviewed in the Introduction, organisational change in museums usually happens in response to, or as a result of, external or internal pressures, such as a need to cut costs, generate more income, increase visitor numbers, realign the organisation to the changing requirements of stakeholders and funders, respond to the impact of external events or become more permeable to community voices. This can necessitate a change in aims, strategy and/or working methods. Most recently, the 2020 Covid-19 pandemic brought all these issues sharply to the fore, with its devastating impact on all walks of life, including museum finances and staffing.

Any organisation – including all its staff, volunteers and stakeholders – needs to understand up front what change may entail and to be prepared for the (often painful and lengthy) process. Table 1.1 shows which aspects of running a museum an organisational change programme might involve, who might be impacted and how.

TABLE 1.1 What organisational change in a museum might involve

What is changing?	Who does it impact?	What might be the impact?
Core mission and aims of the museum	All staff, volunteers, governing body and stakeholders	Changes in roles, job descriptions, working practices, revised strategies and policies
Policies	Potentially all staff, volunteers, governing body and stakeholders	Updating and changing policies on key activities might impact roles, job descriptions and working practices
Governance and leadership	Leaders, governing body, but potentially all staff and volunteers too	For example, change to trust status; changing the nature and remit of trustees and their relationship with the director; including community voices on the governing body; local authority restructuring, including merging departments or moving museums into another department. Some of these will impact on contracts, roles and job descriptions
Staff structures	Potentially all staff and volunteers	Changing staff groupings and who reports to whom; amalgamating departments; amending who is or is not on a senior management team; physically moving staff to different locations
Need to adapt to a sudden and unexpected drop in income	All staff and volunteers	Complete review of aims and mission, staffing levels, structures and activities
Volunteers	Potentially all staff and volunteers	For example, increasing numbers of volunteers working in key areas; changing methods of recruitment of volunteers; changing training, management and supervision of volunteers
Changes as a result of a major capital project	Potentially all staff and volunteers	For example, secondment or reassignment of staff; role changes; temporary closure of some or all of the museum; or relocation
Job descriptions	Potentially all leaders, staff and volunteers	This usually involves negotiations with trade unions and can be a protracted process
Role changes	Potentially all leaders, staff and volunteers	Staff temporarily or permanently reassigned or asked to take on other roles due to, e.g. sickness, maternity/paternity leave, secondment, redundancies

What is changing?	Who does it impact?	What might be the impact?
Cultural change	All staff and volunteers	Changing the values and behaviours of staff and volunteers, e.g. to become more participatory, more commercially minded, to become a learning organisation or to integrate greater equality and diversity
Increasing commercial activities	Leaders, governing body and some staff	Targets to generate set amounts of income from activities might change what the museum is offering, and have an impact on certain roles and ways of working
Broadening audiences	Leaders, governing body and some staff	Targets to diversify visitors: focus on under- or unrepresented groups; change in the nature of museum programming; strategic partnerships with external agencies in order to identify and attract new audiences
Evaluation	All staff and volunteers	Embedding formative evaluation into all activities, and building reflection into all meetings
Sharing decision-making with communities	Leaders, governing body and some staff	For example, setting up participative fora; including community members on the governing body – this impacts ways of working as decision-making involves more people with different perspectives, and can become more complex
Training	Potentially all leaders, governing body, staff and volunteers	Changing the nature of staff continuing professional development; including delivery of training by community partners; or, sometimes, cutting all funding for such training
External voice	Leaders, governing body, some staff	Bringing in critical friends or other external voices to work with key staff groups to provide fresh perspectives and to challenge ways of working
Cutting hours	Potentially all leaders, staff and volunteers	Some or all staff have their hours cut, temporarily or permanently, in times of financial difficulty, through closing the museum early or on one or more days a week, or a decision to open only seasonally
Redundancies	Potentially all leaders, staff and volunteers	Certain staff made redundant for financial reasons, or because the role is no longer needed or has been assimilated, or as a result of restructuring

As the table demonstrates, an organisational change process might involve redundancies, role changes, or cutting hours, but it need not – and it is best to be clear about these points right at the start to ensure that staff understand and buy into the change process.

See also:

7   What is your stimulus for change?
10   Finding common purpose: a shared understanding of change
43   Misunderstanding of change

Note

1   M.M. Ames, 'Introduction', in R.R. Janes, *Museums and the paradox of change: A case study in urgent adaptation* (third edition, Routledge 2013), p. 4.

2

CHANGE TAKES TIME

Change is a continuous process. Most organisational change succeeds after five years, if at all.

Robert Hewison, John Holden and
Samuel Jones, *All Together*[1]

The conventional wisdom is that organisational change takes three to five years at a minimum. In fact, it has been described as a never-ending journey, and it is true that organisational change rarely stops or has a neatly defined end point.

Some commentators on change in the business world think that this is wrong, and that for organisational change in that environment to be successful it must happen rapidly and must create momentum. Yet the evidence from case studies of change in the museum and wider cultural sector clearly demonstrates that it does indeed take time. Even when the need arises to respond to a sudden change in circumstances, which affects funding and staff – such as happened in the wake of the Covid-19 pandemic in 2020 – the actual process of change will take time, although some immediate steps will need to be taken and not deferred.

The most detailed analysis of organisational change in an individual museum – Glenbow Museum in Canada – reveals that it went through discontinuous change for more than a quarter of a century: an initial ten years of tumultuous change which led to more robust finances, a new strategic plan and organisational structure and a more flexible and open way of working. Further changes over seven years by a new CEO were followed by a financial crisis, allegations of mismanagement, and a refocus of its entire mission over five years, which rowed back many of the previous changes. In recent years Glenbow has focused on financial stability and a visitor-centred approach, with the development of new exhibition galleries which have led to record attendances.

> I didn't realise how long change was going to take at Glenbow. It's like gaining weight, it takes a long time to put it on and you can't take it off in two weeks.
>
> Wendy Smith, Glenbow Museum[2]

Glenbow's former CEO points out that change has continued there since his departure, and that any end point is anything but clear as new initiatives and challenges emerge on a daily basis.[3]

At Santa Cruz Museum of Art and History in California, the former Executive Director Nina Simon inherited an organisation in deficit. She instituted a programme of change lasting eight years, changing it into a community-focused resource and thereby transforming the museum's finances. Between 2011 and 2018, visitor numbers rose from 17,000 to 148,000, the annual budget from $700,000 to $3 million – creating a surplus of $400,000 – and the audience profile changed drastically.[4]

In the largest ever programme that focused explicitly on organisational change in the museum sector – the Paul Hamlyn Foundation's *Our Museum: Communities and Museums as Active Partners* – after six years only some of the proposed changes had been properly embedded in organisations making up the cohort. There was evidence of change and progress in other areas, but some aspects still remained a challenge and required further effort, and even more time.[5]

In the wider cultural sector, the Royal Shakespeare Company had a succession of organisational change programmes over 11 years, between 1999 and 2010. An initial crisis in funding, governance and management led to one failed change programme which actually made the crisis worse. This was followed by another major programme focusing on leadership and management, which showed significant progress after two and a half years.[6] By 2014, 450 years since Shakespeare's birth, the Company had opened up significantly to both its local community and its cultural colleagues, starting to create a rich mix of national and international achievements, critical success and local/regional partnerships, while investing significantly in learning and training.

Why does organisational change take so long? There are several interlinked factors.

Change is not necessarily linear or progressive: it can go backwards, as happened in three of the four case studies above. Regression can occur because the change programme is over-optimistic, undermines morale or addresses the wrong problems; sometimes, a change of governance or leadership can stall momentum, or a governing board panics and becomes risk averse, and so the process drags on slowly or peters out.

One of the hardest things to change is the culture of an organisation: it can take years before inertia and traditional ways of working (a 'that's the way we've always done things here' mentality) are transformed across the whole museum.

The financial, political and social environment continues to change around you: so you find yourself constantly responding and adjusting to these external changes, not making real progress. This is why organisational change is more like a process of continuous adaptation.

The cultural sector in general, certainly in the UK, is a step behind the private sector. When a recession bites and public expenditure is cut, there is often a delay before this hits grant aid and cultural programming. This is because of the long lead time for major exhibitions, gallery renewals and theatrical productions, and the revenue funding cycle of sector bodies. This should allow museums to be better prepared for the changes they will have to make as a result of the financial impact of any recession (see Chapter 21: How to sustain change).

However, **museums get side-tracked** from focusing on long-term change by the treadmill of the day job, the delivery of short-term exhibitions and projects. Essentially, museum staff regard change as just another project which has to be fitted in when time allows (see Chapter 47: Other priorities).

Be prepared for the long haul. Embarking on a change programme requires commitment, patience and flexibility. It is a continuing, evolutionary process, not a short-term project, as the next chapter describes. However, as with any journey, arrival or at least improvements in the effectiveness of the museum's functions should be worth the hard work and determination.

See also:

Notes

1   R. Hewison, J. Holden and S. Jones, *All together: A creative approach to organisational change* (Demos 2010), p. 19.
2   Quoted in R.R. Janes, *Museums and the paradox of change: A case study in urgent adaptation* (third edition, Routledge 2013), p. 143.
3   R.R. Janes, *Museums and the paradox of change: A case study in urgent adaptation* (third edition, Routledge 2013), especially pp. 151–91 and 270–71.
4   The best overview is in G. Dunn, 'How Nina Simon reinvented Santa Cruz art', *Good Times* (Santa Cruz), 4 June 2019, goodtimes.sc/cover-stories/nina-simon-reinvented-art-santa-cruz/.
5   P. Bienkowski, *Our Museum: What happened next? A review and further learning two years on* (Paul Hamlyn Foundation 2018), pp. 14–15.
6   R. Hewison, J. Holden and S. Jones, *All together: A creative approach to organisational change* (Demos 2010).

3

THE PROBLEM OF SHORT-TERMISM

The previous chapter stressed that organisational change is long-term and takes years. Yet, ironically for organisations that look after collections for future generations, often museums work with a short-term project mentality. They approach a long-term change programme in just the same way as a short-term project, with short-term goals, deliverables and measures of success.

This is understandable, since most museum funding is either project-funding for delivering predefined outputs – exhibitions, events, visitor numbers – or annual or triennial budget rounds which must be bid for at regular intervals. This leads to constant pressure to report immediate success to funders (and a reluctance to report failure), producing positive reports of short-term wins that act as advocacy to secure further funding.

It is not unusual for a number of projects to be delivered across a museum by different groups of staff and volunteers – sometimes on short-term project contracts – with little connection between them and not always sharing learning or feeding into the corporate memory and taken forward to future projects. You might be doing excellent project work, but with a lack of overall direction and no sense that you are doing things differently as you learn from mistakes.

> The area where we fall down is legacy and long-term. We work intensively with groups and move on. That's the issue with project funding – you move on to the next thing.
>
> Anonymous museum staff member[1]

It is essential to shift away from this short-term project mentality when under-taking a change programme. Change cannot be organised, staffed or even funded as a project. While it is useful to include some quick wins that boost morale, especially when facing a crisis, you must keep your eye on the long term: what you are aiming for, and your ultimate measures of success.

A change programme requires longer-term strategic planning that involves the organisation as a whole, and encourages buy-in from all staff and the sharing of ideas, learning, hopes and fears. It is useful to model the proposed change in advance, to clarify your long-term aims and the individual activities that, over the years, will accumulate to achieve that overall change. During the change process, things will not always go to plan, and it is important to have mechanisms of formative evalu-ation in place to learn from those mistakes as they happen, and either get back on track or deliberately change your direction (see Chapter 49: Tracking your change journey). This is a luxury that most short-term projects do not have, largely because much of the evaluation is done at the end, when it is too late to alter anything.

The key point to clarify to all of those involved in the change process is that it is not a short-term project to be fitted in around other projects. Many programmes of organisational change are, fundamentally, reappraisals of ways of working for the long term. While projects and budgets typically last a few months, a year, or excep-tionally three years, the vision for organisational change needs to extend far beyond that, to five or ten years in the future: what sort of museum do we want to be by then and why, and what will that look and feel like?

See also:

9   Why modelling change can help
10   Finding common purpose
37   Overcoming project mentality

Note

1   Quoted in B. Lynch, *Whose cake is it anyway? A collaborative investigation into engagement and participation in 12 museums and galleries in the UK* (Paul Hamlyn Foundation 2011), p. 18.

4

SMALL CHANGES ADD UP

Change is often divided into two main types: transformational or incremental. Transformational (or radical) change affects an organisation's structure and culture. Incremental change modifies or adjusts the status quo through relatively simple and minor changes, but does not affect existing structures or fundamentally alter current methods of working.

An alternative approach – small changes add up – is becoming increasingly common in the museum and cultural sector, and combines the advantages of both transformational and incremental change. Small improvements and changes in many different areas, across the whole museum, add up to significant transformation. Although each individual change might be small, cumulatively they can lead to big overall change and alter an organisation's course and how it is perceived externally, thereby adding up to more than the sum of their parts and having greater impact.

Experimentation and constant small-scale innovations help change to happen.
Robert Hewison, John Holden and Samuel Jones, *All Together*[1]

In the museum sector, the term 'small changes add up' was popularised by the Paul Hamlyn Foundation programme *Our Museum: Communities and Museums as Active Partners*. Five key areas of museum practice and management were identified as particularly critical – these were the areas where small changes could be made, which added up to overall transformational change.[2]

Changes in governance and leadership, including developing distributed leadership by delegating and empowering staff.

Staff professional development: developing staff buy-in to change, supporting champions and influencers of change to counter staff resistance.

Developing external partnerships, especially with communities and agencies in the voluntary and charitable sector, who make excellent strategic partners for museums.

Evaluation: recognition that organisational change benefits from a rigorous approach to qualitative evaluation based on shared reflection.

The importance of the external voice, especially critical friends, to bring fresh and independent perspectives to the process of change and help ensure that difficult issues are addressed and not avoided.

Similarly, the changes that added up at Glenbow Museum in Canada over ten years included work on long-term strategy, mission and vision, values, management, sustainable funding, cost-cutting, and introduction of both quantitative and qualitative performance measures.[3]

The insightful analysis of the organisational change process at the Royal Shakespeare Company concludes that there are many advantages in undertaking small changes on a continuous, experimental basis:[4]

- Small changes are less threatening than transformational change.
- They can be stopped if the change becomes problematic.
- Small-scale change is easier to slow down, speed up or extend across the whole organisation than large-scale change.
- It is less expensive than a large-scale change programme.
- Small changes create momentum and stimulus through quick wins.
- It focuses energy and develops confidence without staff feeling they are being pushed into something new and uncomfortable.
- Small-scale change and quick wins provide frequent opportunities for celebration.
- Small changes acknowledge that different parts of an organisation move at a different pace, and that not everyone is persuaded of the need for change at the same time.

See also:

12   Explore and test – the value of pilot projects
49   Tracking your change journey

Notes

1   R. Hewison, J. Holden and S. Jones, *All together: A creative approach to organisational change* (Demos 2010), p. 127.
2   P. Bienkowski, *No longer us and them: How to change into a participatory museum and gallery – Learning from the Our Museum programme* (Paul Hamlyn Foundation 2016), pp. 19–39.
3   R.R. Janes, *Museums and the paradox of change: A case study in urgent adaptation* (third edition, Routledge 2013), pp. 13–43.
4   R. Hewison, J. Holden and S. Jones, *All together: A creative approach to organisational change* (Demos 2010), p. 127.

5

CHANGE IS EVERYONE'S JOB

Although change is often imposed by directors with little consultation, in practice they know they cannot do it on their own, nor do they want to do so. Being a director is a lonely role. Directors need the support of their staff, governing bodies and external individuals and organisations. Many change projects will only succeed if individual staff and volunteers change their daily behaviours and start doing their jobs in a new way. While directors can 'walk the talk' to show models of behaviour, they cannot do the whole job alone.

> Change can't just affect one small area, it filters out across everything. . . . It really requires buy-in from everybody.
>
> Sally Noall, Tate St Ives[1]

The James Irvine Foundation's programme across ten organisations on transforming engagement programming found that, initially, change programmes started with a core group of people but soon discovered that success was dependent on the participation and commitment of other staff. Over time, they found that buy-in from virtually all staff was necessary for change to succeed, even those apparently less affected by the work in their day-to-day roles.[2]

The big lesson here is that change has to come from across the whole organisation. Directors need to treat staff (and volunteers) as responsible adults, involve them in understanding and managing the change process from the very beginning and all staff need to assume responsibility for improving things.

Change is not just the director's or someone else's job. Whether those impacted by change like it or not, and whether they are aware of it or not, it involves everyone, inside and outside the museum. It is everyone's job. From the top to the bottom, inside and out, governing bodies, directors, staff, volunteers, community partners, strategic sector bodies and funders all have a role in the process of change. It takes time, patience and commitment from everyone. The challenge is often to find out what each individual's role within the change process is in practice.

The role of governing bodies, strategic sector organisations and funders in a change process is fairly obvious and straightforward. They make the strategic decision to embark on change, provide support, training and mentoring to leaders and staff and occasionally explicit funding towards change. It is important to build buy-in from the governing body to support a change programme. All members of this board must fully understand their role as active supporters of the process. They should also know what to say, and what not to say, if staff approach them directly about their own concerns (see also Chapter 39: Communicating change).

Occasionally, of course, not everyone on a governing body is committed to change, or to a particular direction of change. Consequently, an important element of building buy-in is to consider the membership, skills and values of the board, looking for opportunities to strategically remove uncommitted board members and to bring in new ones. However, as the director, you must plan ahead so that a succession plan can achieve this without it looking like Machiavellian moves on your part (see Chapters 8: Balancing conflicting priorities, and 15: Governance and change).[3]

> Those who will implement the changes must be intimately involved in creating the plan, which means this work cannot be done successfully from the top down.
>
> Robert Janes, *Museums and the Paradox of Change*[4]

The proactive role of staff and volunteers in change is less well understood. It is often the case that individual staff members and volunteers feel slightly helpless and blown about by the winds of change, accepting as their inevitable lot that they can do nothing about it. But it is counterproductive to try to resist change, and readiness for change can prove invaluable to staff. The worst thing you can do is to be constantly negative, as is the case with some museum professionals.

According to Daniel Pink, people are motivated to work well and have the greatest satisfaction in their work not by money, but when they have a sense of common purpose, freedom to control their work as much as possible and know they are doing their job well.[5] Change is everyone's responsibility, and any staff member or volunteer can, and should, be prepared to contribute to the process. It is important to stand up and offer to be part of it. In this way, rather than letting change happen to you, everyone can become a proactive change agent.

So what can individual staff members do? Much of it is about their own understanding of the change process and how it might impact them and the museum. There are simple actions such as asking for help, support and advice from a line manager or a human resources department. Mostly, though, it is about taking personal responsibility, and asking themselves the question: *what is my own role in the change process?* One of the things people struggle with most during organisational change is communication – trying to find out what is really going on (see Chapter 39: Communicating change). You should actively seek out information about what is happening and how it affects you, and not just expect to be told. The best way to deal with this is to have multiple ways of sharing and receiving information, with different colleagues across the museum. Setting up action learning sets is a good way to take control – to discuss what the proposed change entails and prepare for it, share experiences, fears, ideas, offer support – and to feed those ideas back to the director and other staff. In this way, everyone becomes a change agent and facilitator of the process.[6]

There are now plenty of resources about organisational change in the museum sector (see *Resources to Help You* and *Useful Publications* at the end of this book). Staff and volunteers can look at these themselves, and pass them around to colleagues, directors, senior management teams and governing bodies. The online films listed in the *Resources to Help You* section can be used to stimulate discussion and share thoughts about the nature and impact of change at staff meetings, lunchtime discussion sessions or action learning sets. You might suggest a presentation to all staff from someone who has run or been involved in a change programme – what went well and not so well, and the challenges they faced. This can take place within your own museum; however, if you feel constrained or disempowered from doing something like this, you can ask an external support body to schedule such a talk at a neutral venue – for example, in the United Kingdom, a regional museum federation or museum development officer (similar networks exist in other countries). Ideally, you should arrange visits to other organisations which have gone through change.

Chapter 52 in this book is about external voices and critical friends, who can help unearth difficult topics that the museum finds it hard to talk about and who also have a vital role in the change process. Some staff and volunteers may feel that it is difficult to express worries and uncomfortable truths within their organisation and therefore to have any real impact on the change process, and there are directors who see external voices as a threat. Nevertheless, external voices can come from several sources: they can be peers from other museums, commissioned critical friends, funders, evaluators, community partners or artists. This is where staff and volunteers can have some influence – by proposing an external voice, perhaps from another museum that has gone through a change process, or a community partner, to give a different perspective on the change you are going through. The presence of an external voice can open up a useful discussion involving everyone about the change going on at the museum.

See also:

10   Finding common purpose: a shared understanding of change
32   Supporting staff and volunteers during change

Notes

1 S. Noall, 'Ideas and bravery', in M. Miller, R. Moilliet and E. Daly (eds.), *Circuit – Test, Risk, Change: Young people, youth organisations and galleries working together* (Tate and Paul Hamlyn Foundation 2019), pp. 160–61.

2 S. Lee and K. Gean, *The Engagement Revolution: A study of strategic organizational transformation in 10 California arts nonprofits* (James Irvine Foundation 2017), p. 36.

3 S. Lee and K. Gean, *The Engagement Revolution: A study of strategic organizational transformation in 10 California arts nonprofits* (James Irvine Foundation 2017), p. 33.

4 R.R. Janes, *Museums and the paradox of change: A case study in urgent adaptation* (third edition, Routledge 2013), p. 74.

5 D.H. Pink, *Drive* (Canongate Books 2011).

6 See also the list of practical actions for developing personal agency in the museum, whatever the role or position, suggested in R.R. Janes, *Museums and the paradox of change: A case study in urgent adaptation* (third edition, Routledge 2013), pp. 360–62. These range from asking to attend a board meeting to questioning leaders why you are doing what you are doing. Realistically, though, some of the proposed actions are about structure and line management and beyond the control of individual staff members.

PART 2
Preparing for change

> It must be considered that there is nothing more difficult to carry out, nor more doubtful of success, nor more dangerous to handle, than to initiate a new order of things.
>
> Machiavelli, *The Prince*

A crucial part of organisational change is preparing the museum or gallery – and its leaders, staff and volunteers – for change. Are the organisation and its staff ready for change, and can they sustain it over a long period? Preparation for change can also help to clarify the drivers and aims of the change and begin to create a shared vision. This has the added value for a director or governing body of identifying both champions of change and potential resisters.

Preparing for change includes readiness to be open to different perspectives and trying things out, and being prepared for the chaos that is likely to happen at some point in the process. Organisational change can be a major upheaval: staff may be under pressure to work in radically different ways and may react unpredictably and negatively. Anticipation is the key to chaos not overwhelming the organisation.

6

ARE YOU READY FOR CHANGE?

As change is, by its very nature, disruptive and can be destabilising, before you embark upon change, or launch a change programme, experience has shown that it is helpful to carry out a health check on the organisation, to assess if you are ready for this change.[1] If the need for change has been acknowledged within the museum, then the nature of what needs to happen should become clearer as a result of such a health check. This will also give you advance warning of potential pitfalls awaiting you and frailties in your organisation which the change process can address and aim to strengthen. In addition, it can clarify key areas of weakness which may undermine the process and the positive impact of change.

A basic health check may comprise:

- a mini business plan
- a self-administered governance review
- an effectiveness review of the leadership and managerial processes (this will depend on your category of institution, e.g. if you are an independent museum, then this would include the effectiveness of your trustee board and its partnership with the executive staff/volunteer workforce)
- possibly a staff meeting/discussion or a round-robin email asking for comments to specific questions, e.g. about visitor reactions or staff skills and development needs.

Your starting point here should be your 'Why?' (see Chapter 10) – why your museum exists and what it exists to do. The purpose of your change programme will be to put your museum into a better position to fulfil its mission, whether financially or in terms of staffing, structure, partnerships or ways of working. The key thing is to use what you learn in preparing for the change process and respond to any concerns your staff/volunteers raise as a result of the reviews.

Consider how you may communicate in the coming weeks. You should take into account staff and volunteers who do not work full time Monday to Friday, and who may not be able to attend single briefings/staff discussions. You might need to repeat some briefings to include everyone. Consider introducing new methods of communication and, above all, ensure that your communications strategy is inclusive (see Chapter 39 on communicating change).

As a result of these exercises and assessments, you can judge if your museum is ready for change. At its best, a systematic health check helps clarify aims and can create a shared vision in which everyone feels involved.

See also:

10 Finding common purpose
12 Explore and test – the value of pilot projects
39 Communicating change, internally and externally

Note

1 P. Bienkowski, *Our Museum: What happened next? A review and further learning two years on* (Paul Hamlyn Foundation 2018), p. 16.

7

WHAT IS YOUR STIMULUS FOR CHANGE?

The need to change is usually a response to different external pressures, as outlined in the Introduction. Often these pressures will lead to, or be caused by, a change of leadership: director, chief executive of parent body, or chair. This may have been stimulated by a new vision for the organisation, changes in funding or a capital project which brings investment and requires new ways of working as a result.

Across the world, museums and galleries in some countries have now modernised and become more outward-looking and user-focused, but some are still out of step not only with the thought-leadership of the sector but with what the public expect and want. In these cases, wholesale change and its subsequent upheaval are required to update the organisation.

This type of change is likely to be director-led, supported and encouraged by the governing body who may have appointed the person to achieve the change they require. This can be positive change and is often welcomed by many members of staff and stakeholders. A positive outlook at the start and a positive stimulus for the change will make a significant difference to how it is received and supported by staff and volunteers, and how effective the change may be ultimately.

If the change is self-imposed, it may be as a result of the health checks or reviews carried out (see Chapters 6 and 12); if so, you should be in control of the process and the timescale. If change is imposed from an external source – central or local government, a change in governance, cuts in funding or enforced job losses impacting on leadership and operation – then as the museum leader you may not be in control of all of it (see Chapter 24: Involving stakeholders in the change process).

Cuts in museum funding often have their origins in a disconnect with funders' agendas (this is especially true with regard to local authority funding in the UK). Museum professionals have a fierce pride in their work and a strong belief in the impact of their organisation and of museums in general. Presenting these beliefs to some governing bodies (e.g. central or local government in the UK) does not always go down well and is often misunderstood and resented. Making funders feel like they need to be on the defensive to justify their actions of setting savings targets does not make for a productive relationship. Museum professionals' belief in the power of museums[1] and their understanding of their impact can easily make them at odds with elected politicians who might have different priorities and believe they can see the wider picture.

The UK Museums Association is the world's oldest professional membership for those who work in museums, and its Code of Ethics[2] is admired and referred to internationally, especially in those countries without their own codes of museum ethics. First created as two separate codes (one for museum workers and one for institutions), the Code is built into the UK Museums Accreditation standards. This epitomises the clash of principles often inherent in change programmes that have been stimulated by a need for new and different types of funding (see also Chapter 8 on balancing conflicting priorities). Many practitioners have used the Code to guide difficult decisions in their careers. But it is unwise for it to be a stick with which to beat funders who have larger financial worries. Staff should be encouraged to use the spirit of the Code to respect their funders/employers and try to understand why the museum is being required to change in a particular way. This respect is the basis for a productive relationship.

Negative change is stimulated by activity such as job losses, global crises or funding cuts, and this is usually externally imposed. The process here would then happen in an atmosphere of negativity with many – or all – of those involved being reluctant to engage with the change. In these circumstances, those affected may be openly resistant and seek to sabotage and derail the process.

Externally imposed change may also be a result of circumstances outside your museum's control, such as terrorism, natural disasters or medical crises. In these situations, the museum may be fighting for its survival, so the response from the staff is also likely to be more supportive given the external circumstances.

See also:

21   How to sustain change
28   Embracing risk
31   Countering resistance

Notes

1 E.g. *Museums Change Lives* (Museums Association 2017), museumsassociation.org/museums-change-lives/the-impact-of-museums.
2 *Code of Ethics* (Museums Association 2015), museumsassociation.org/ethics/code-of-ethics.

8

BALANCING CONFLICTING PRIORITIES

A change process is an opportunity to radically shift, or at least rebalance, the priorities of the museum. But what can you do when different constituencies or stakeholders, both internal and external, believe in different goals, and each sees the change process as an opportunity to advance its own agenda? For example, local authorities, funders, community organisations, governing boards and various groups of staff may all be pulling in different directions in terms of priorities – so how can you strike a balance between people who want one kind of change against those who want another, to ensure their opinions are integrated and that people feel listened to and not alienated from the organisation?

In general, conflicting priorities tend to fall into one of two groups: prioritising means (especially financial resources) over ends, and conflict over different, possibly incompatible ends.

The tension between ends and means

Museums and galleries are increasingly concerned about long-term financial sustainability and income generation, and in many cases that is the driver for change (see Chapter 7). A financial crisis as a catalyst for change is usually caused by withdrawal of, or cuts in, funding streams, sometimes over several years so that the organisation suffers long-term financial decline and an uncertain future.[1] In many instances, the response is change programmes that lead to new business plans, restructurings, redundancies and a stronger focus on fundraising and generating income. They do not always lead to new coherent mission statements, as many short-term money-saving ideas are often implemented at knee-jerk speed.

What often then happens is that the generation of income becomes such an overwhelming priority that it becomes an end in itself. Staff members are given individual income-generation targets that they regard as a key part of their job, taking precedence over many other activities.

It is important to keep a sense of perspective, and to remember that sustainability is not the museum's reason for existing. Generating income may be a means of the organisation surviving, but it is a means: it is not the purpose of the organisation (see Chapter 10 for your 'Why?'). This is a typical 'what-how?' question: *what* is the museum here to do, and *how* is it going to resource it? Activities such as generating income are a *how*, not a *what*. Elevating them to a *what* distorts the aims of the museum. If the generation of income takes over as an overriding aim, then it is legitimate to ask whether the museum is worth sustaining.

Ultimately, therefore, the question for many change programmes is not primarily about prioritising revenue generation but about refocusing the purpose and approach of the museum so that it addresses community and stakeholder needs and is able to attract sustainable support and funding.[2] In some cases, the only solution to declining funds has been to switch to an explicit policy of community participation, which is seen as essential for financial sustainability.

> These organizations felt a mandate to make themselves more financially sustainable and recognized that they needed to become more relevant to those who weren't well represented in their current audience base in order to survive.
> Sarah Lee and Katherine Gean, *The Engagement Revolution*[3]

In Sweden, for example, diversifying audiences and reflecting their interests was a requirement for renewed government funding for some museums.[4] In other cases, however, museum finance directors or funders such as local authorities or central government are not supportive of community engagement as they think it does not generate sufficient income. Here there is an expectation that such work requires separate funding or it is at risk, thus undermining the strategic imperative to become more relevant.[5] This is a classic case of prioritising *means* over *ends*: if community engagement has been agreed upon as a strategic priority and is key to making the museum more relevant and sustainable in the longer term, then *means* should be identified to resource it.

It is true that some community engagement activities are targeted at very small numbers of participants, and assessments on purely financial parameters often criticise this as a poor use of resources and not viable in the long term. But this needs to be weighed against the risk of *not* doing this work with the museum slowly sliding into irrelevancy (see Chapter 17). Moreover, as the examples at the end of this chapter show, community input is vital to help the museum develop its long-term strategy, and these collaborative processes can regularly involve considerable numbers (see also Chapter 25: Community partnerships and change).

The best way of addressing any tension between *means* and *ends* is to confront it head on and discuss it at the board and senior management team level: identify what are, ultimately, *ends* (e.g. impact on communities, or x number of visitors attending y number of events each year), and what are the *means* to achieve these (e.g. revenue generation, fundraising targets), and then tease out what might be tensions between them in practice, in terms of which activities or programmes should be supported and how.

The management team at Tyne & Wear Archives & Museums, a large local authority service in the north of England, confronted this as part of their change process during the *Our Museum* programme. At a workshop devoted to this topic, they decided that there was no tension between income generation and participation in principle, but acknowledged that in practice it was sometimes difficult to weigh them up when making decisions about which activities to carry out. They recognised that different audiences or events generate different levels of income. In cases where participatory work generates less income or even makes a loss, their strategy was to cover the cost by other activities. This so-called Robin Hood strategy paid for high priority 'poorer' activities by using income from the 'richer' activities. Their solution, therefore, was that not every individual activity has to justify itself by being self-sustaining.

Such an approach demonstrates that activities that are strategic imperatives need not be penalised for their lack of income-generating potential. Because they are high priority ends – the reason why the museum exists in the first place – the means can often be underwritten from other activities that are higher earning. Likewise, activities that generate higher income should not always be prioritised as a matter of course, if it means that other strategic imperatives cannot be carried out as a result. Means should not trump ends: generating income should never be treated as a priority on the same level as, for example, making an impact on your community. They are priorities *of a different kind*, with the former serving the latter. If you clearly distinguish between the two, and ensure the whole team understands the distinction and the consequences, it will make decision-making easier and more strategic.

Reaching consensus over conflicting ends

Another type of balancing problem occurs when different constituencies are aligned with different, seemingly incompatible goals. In the UK, it is not uncommon for tensions to arise around whether to prioritise audience numbers through a programme of exhibitions and events, or make an impact on people's lives by working in partnership with community organisations or to become a centre of academic excellence with a world-class collection in a particular discipline. In the USA, there is often tension between, on the one hand, the ties of museums to the art market – especially through the influence of collectors who might be trustees – regardless of whether such alliances serve the needs of the broader community, and, on the other hand, museum staff who support increased community-based initiatives that have little to do with the art market. This situation is exacerbated when revenue models depend on keeping collector-trustees on board to compensate for the lack of government funding. In such cases, a director needs to maintain the buy-in and support of staff, curators and trustees, and the situation can be akin to treading a razor's edge in terms of balancing conflicting priorities.

This variety of ideas of what a museum is for, or about, has been thrown into global perspective in recent years by the negative reaction to a new definition of a museum proposed by ICOM (the International Council of Museums) in July 2019. The proposed definition called museums democratising and inclusive places which should contribute to human dignity, social justice, global equality and planetary wellbeing. Critics called it an ideological manifesto and a 'coup' against the traditional idea of a museum which is about stewardship, collections, preservation and exhibition. These conflicting understandings of the role of museums are being played out at individual museums every day across the whole world.

What is really at issue here is the process of agreeing on the goals of the museum, their 'Why?': who is involved in that process, what goals are prioritised and for whose benefit (and assessing whether some goals really are incompatible with others). The smaller and more restricted the group that decides goals, the more likelihood that there will be constituencies who feel that their interests and perspectives have not been taken into account. A strategy agreed upon in isolation by a governing body and a director will always be in danger of not attracting a broad consensus – and without broad consensus, any change is unlikely to succeed (see Chapter 44: Change is imposed).

In many ways, the solution to these problems is very simple: increasing the diversity of voices involved in an open and honest process of setting goals increases the likelihood of reaching consensus. Even if some of those involved disagree with group recommendations, they may be more easily reconciled to the outcomes because there has been an opportunity for all to argue and justify their positions in good faith. Directors and trustees sometimes counter that it is their job to take such strategic decisions, as that is what they were appointed to do. However, they still remain the ultimate decision-makers, as they are the ones who facilitate the process of goal-setting and sign off on its recommendations.

So, who should be involved in the process of setting strategic goals, and what form might that process take? Where a collaborative process of strategic goal-setting has been carried out successfully, it has involved the director and senior managers, trustees, staff, volunteers, communities and stakeholders – literally, everyone with an interest and stake in the museum. Everyone's priorities go into the pot to be argued over and justified (see also Chapters 5 and 11).

Such collaborative processes have been used for new/redeveloped museums, for setting new strategic directions and for annual reappraisals of goals.

- **Participatory fora**: for its redevelopment, St Fagan's National Museum of History, part of Amgueddfa Cymru-National Museum Wales, worked with 200 organisations across Wales in the public, voluntary and charitable sectors to help shape and develop the planning process and strategy. These included agencies covering homelessness, unemployment, disability, ethnic minorities, substance misuse, mental health issues, and working with non-English speakers. Their strategic input was channelled through a range of participatory fora on topics such as diversity, participation, formal and informal learning, and youth involvement.

- **Collaborative consultation**: the new strategic direction for the Museum of East Anglian Life came out of a consultative process of workshops involving staff, volunteers, trustees, stakeholders and communities. There was a genuine sharing of ideas, and a feeling that everyone had a voice and saw it represented in the strategy that emerged.

> Communities were involved in workshops to develop our new strategy. It was a collaborative process which led to consensus: everyone felt involved and their ideas were represented in our forward plan.
>
> Jenny Cousins, Museum of East Anglian Life[6]

- **Regular discussion events**: many museums now involve external voices in regular discussion about strategy and programming. Tyne & Wear Archives & Museums, aiming to move to a strategy that reflects local and community needs, experimented with an annual 'People's Parliament' attended by staff and community members, to discuss future strategy and priorities. Glasgow Museums holds a regular discussion forum, the Creative Café, linked to its planning cycles, which brings together staff and external partners to share and shape ideas about future work.

These collaborative approaches aim at consensus around the strategic direction of museums, rather than directors or governing bodies imposing strategy unilaterally. They are an important step on the way to achieving a shared understanding of change that everyone can support – which is crucial to ensure that the change succeeds and is sustainable (see Chapter 10: Finding common purpose).

See also:

6   Are you ready for change?
10   Finding common purpose: a shared understanding of change

Note

1   One English local authority museum reported cuts of 69 per cent between 2010 and 2017: see *Cuts Survey 2015* (Museums Association 2015), p. 5. For documented financial

crises at Glenbow Museum in Canada, Oakland Museum of California and Santa Cruz Museum of Art and History, see R.R. Janes, *Museums and the paradox of change: A case study in urgent adaptation* (third edition, Routledge 2013), pp. 14 and 195 for Glenbow and Oakland, and S. Lee and K. Gean, *The Engagement Revolution: A study of strategic organizational transformation in 10 California arts nonprofits* (James Irvine Foundation 2017), p. 48 for Santa Cruz. For museums and financial crises in general, see K. Lindqvist, 'Museum finances: Challenges beyond economic crises', *Museum Management and Curatorship* 27(1) (2012), pp. 1–15.

2 P. Bienkowski, *No longer us and them: How to change into a participatory museum and gallery – Learning from the Our Museum programme* (Paul Hamlyn Foundation 2016), p. 5; N. Simon, *The art of relevance* (Museum 2.0 2016).

3 S. Lee and K. Gean, *The Engagement Revolution: A study of strategic organizational transformation in 10 California arts nonprofits* (James Irvine Foundation 2017), p. 24.

4 C. Lagerkvist, 'The Museum of World Culture: A "glocal" museum of a new kind', in K. Goodnow and H. Akman (eds.), *Scandinavian Museums and cultural diversity* (Berghahn Books 2008), pp. 89–100.

5 P. Bienkowski, *No longer us and them: How to change into a participatory museum and gallery – Learning from the Our Museum programme* (Paul Hamlyn Foundation 2016), p. 42.

6 Quoted in *Power to the people: A self-assessment framework for participatory practice* (Museums Association 2018), p. 13.

9

WHY MODELLING CHANGE CAN HELP

It always helps to have a plan up front. Change management models help you to organise solutions, plan for potential problems, and keep your team and stakeholders informed of progress. Most importantly, they clarify the connection between your current activities and your long-term aims – what you want to achieve through the change. The plan may well change – in fact, it almost certainly will – but it gives you a sense of direction and helps monitor how far you have travelled.

There are many different ways of modelling change, and you should choose one that suits your circumstances and that you – and your staff – feel comfortable with. Here is a brief overview of the six change models most commonly used in museums and galleries.

Theory of change

This may sound like the definitive answer to managing change but, in fact, the Theory of Change (TOC) is simply one approach. TOC can be a useful tool to identify what steps need to be taken to achieve a long-term goal, articulate it clearly, assess the time and resources available, and document it systematically.[1]

There are five steps to creating a theory of change that work backwards from the ultimate goal:

- Identify a long-term goal.
- Identify what elements (or preconditions) need to be in place to achieve that goal.
- Identify your basic assumptions about the context.
- Identify the interventions that your change programme will perform to create these elements.

- Develop indicators for each element that will be used to assess the performance of the interventions.

These are usually shown diagrammatically in a chart, in logical relationship to one another.

Logic modelling

A logic model is usually a graphic depiction of the relationships between the resources, activities, outputs and outcomes of a programme. It is 'logical' because it assesses the 'if-then' causal relationship between the different elements of the programme.

- **If** resources are available to the programme
- **Then** programme activities can be implemented.
- **If** programme activities are implemented successfully
- **Then** certain outputs and outcomes can be expected.

A good logic model will present a picture of how your initiative is supposed to work and make an explicit, often visual, statement of the activities that will bring about change and expected results. A logic model can be used to evaluate a programme, initiative, project or an organisation's complete work.

It is usually tabulated to show the link between resources, activities, and short-, medium- and long-term outcomes, as in Table 9.1.

Kotter eight-step process for leading change

John Kotter's eight-step process for leading change focuses on continuous adaptation across the whole organisation. It is designed to guide organisations in thinking about delivering change and seeing it through. It recognises that between 70 and 75 per cent of all major change programmes in organisations fail, because they do not take the holistic approach required to see change through. Kotter identified why change fails and proposed his eight-step solution to success:[2]

- Too much complacency > **create** a sense of urgency.
- No sustainable coalition > **build** the guiding coalition.

TABLE 9.1 Example of a logic model

Resources	Activities	Short-term outcomes	Medium-term outcomes	Long-term outcomes
For example, funding, staff time	For example, staff training, reflective workshops	For example, staff understand the reasons for change	For example, staff contribute to the change programme	For example, staff are working in a different way

- No understanding of a need for a vision > **form** a change vision.
- Failure to communicate vision > **enlist** a volunteer army.
- Allowing obstacles to hinder vision > **enable** action by removing barriers.
- Not planning for short-term wins > **generate** short-term wins.
- Declaring a victory too soon > **sustain** acceleration.
- Failure to consolidate change in the culture > **institute** change.

McKinsey 7S framework

The McKinsey 7S framework underlines that you cannot change any part of your organisation in isolation. The framework involves seven interdependent factors:

- **Strategy**: the long-term plan of the museum.
- **Structure**: the way the museum is structured and who reports to whom.
- **Systems**: the daily activities and procedures that staff engage in to get the job done.
- **Shared values**: the core values of the museum – often but not always explicitly negotiated with staff.
- **Style**: the style of leadership adopted.
- **Staff**: the employees and volunteers and their general capabilities.
- **Skills**: the actual skills and competencies of the staff and volunteers.

The first three are 'hard' elements which are easier to define, and which management can directly influence. The remaining four are 'soft' elements which are more difficult to describe, and are more influenced by the culture of the organisation. But they are all interdependent, with shared values being central to the development of all of them – for example, if those shared values change for any reason, then it will affect how everything else is done.

The model is based on the theory that, for an organisation to perform well, these seven elements need to be aligned and mutually reinforcing. So the model can be used to help identify what needs to be changed or realigned to improve performance. Changes in any one area affect all the others.

Lewin three-stage model and force field analysis

Kurt Lewin (1890–1947), a pioneer of organisational psychology, identified three stages to a change process, using the analogy of an organisation as a block of ice:[3]

- **Unfreeze**: preparing for change, overcoming inertia and dismantling the existing mind-set.
- **Change**: implementation, confusion, transition.
- **Refreeze**: institutionalising change and making it permanent.

In Lewin's force field analysis, a situation is held in balance by the interaction of two opposing sets of forces – those seeking to promote change (driving forces) and those attempting to maintain the status quo (restraining forces). For change to occur, this balance must be disturbed, either by increasing the driving, positive forces for change or by reducing restraining forces. Many organisations complete a force field analysis to identify influences and situations that work for and against the desired change, using the analysis as a practical change model.[4]

Appreciative Inquiry

Appreciative Inquiry (AI) focuses on building organisations around what works, rather than looking to fix what doesn't. Its methodology focuses on having conversations and asking questions, in this way increasing capacity for collaboration and change.[5]

AI's framework for change or development is the 5D cycle:

- **Definition**: choose the focus of inquiry and frame it in a positive rather than negative way, highlighting aspirations, not problems.
- **Discovery**: assess the organisation's strengths, capabilities, resources and assets – its 'positive core'.
- **Dream**: explore hopes and dreams of the ideal organisation, imagining 'what could be'.
- **Design**: construct in detail the vision explored in the dream phase.
- **Deliver/Destiny**: how to deliver the design and embed it in the organisation.

See also:

12   Explore and test – the value of pilot projects
49   Tracking your change journey

Notes

1   TOC tools and training materials are available on the Theory of Change website, www.theoryofchange.org.
2   J.P. Kotter, *Leading change* (Harvard Business Press 1996), updated and enhanced in Kotter, *Accelerate: Building strategic agility for a faster-moving world* (Harvard Business Review Publishing 2014).
3   K. Lewin, *Resolving social conflicts and field theory in social science* (American Psychological Association 1997).
4   For Lewin's model applied to the museum sector, see R. Sandell, 'Social inclusion, the museum and the dynamics of sectoral change', *Museum and Society* 1(1) (2003), pp. 45–62.
5   S. Lewis, J. Passmore and S. Cantore, *Appreciative Inquiry for change management: Using AI to facilitate organizational development* (second edition, Kogan Page 2016).

10

FINDING COMMON PURPOSE

A shared understanding of change

It is crucial to explain and discuss the purpose and likely impact of the change within the organisation before the start of the process, so that everyone understands the reason for change and is prepared for it. There are several points to clarify:

- whether the need for change is a result of political or community pressure, a new director, or a funding stream that encourages participatory practice
- whether the objective is to make the organisation more permeable to community voices, change governance, share decision-making, policies, values and behaviours, or change staff roles and job descriptions
- how long the change process is likely to take (three years? five years?).

To maximise support and understanding of change, these topics should be widely discussed beforehand throughout the whole organisation.

When the Association of Independent Museums carried out widespread market research with UK museums in 2015, they found the greatest risk to museums prospering was their lack of clarity of purpose. Asked why their museum existed and what it did, staff, volunteers, directors, trustees and other governing bodies all gave different answers. So establishing clarity of purpose became the first Hallmark of Prospering Museums.[1]

Equally, getting everyone in the organisation to understand the reasons why change is needed and to support the desired outcomes is a significant step towards achieving it. As a leader you will know why change is needed, but it must be a shared vision for a common purpose if it is to succeed and have a positive impact.

This also has the advantage of ensuring that the museum leader can articulate the change process and speak eloquently about the impact they are seeking. The authors have both seen change not being clearly explained and subsequently many of those involved not being aware that change was either needed or expected.

Your starting point for identifying common purpose must be finding your 'Why?' (see Chapter 6: Are you ready for change?) – so a first step may be to articulate why your museum exists and what it exists to do.[2] Your change will be seeking to place your museum in a position to fulfil your mission, whether this originates from its founders long ago, from legislation, or from a present member of staff such as the director or a current trustee. Finding your 'Why?' should involve everyone in the organisation, as every aspect of the museum's work should feed into the outcome. This can be done through discussions, workshops, focus groups or action learning sets (see examples at the end of Chapter 8). Involving all staff/volunteers as well as community partners and stakeholders is a position of strength from which to launch your change programme.

Not only must the need for change be shared but the process and impact – what the change will mean for day-to-day work – must be understood too. Finding a common purpose is an effective means to win hearts and minds. This should ease the change process and can identify both active supporters – who may become champions of the change – and blockers – who may seek to sabotage the process. For a museum leader, being able to identify both as early as possible could be key to the success of the change programme.

See also:

8   Balancing conflicting priorities
29   Don't be afraid to report problems or 'failure'
34   Champions of change
43   Misunderstanding of change

Notes

1   AIM Hallmarks, www.aim-museums.co.uk/aim-hallmarks/.
2   See S. Sinek, *Find your why: A practical guide for discovering purpose for you and your team* (Penguin 2017).

11

BE OPEN TO CHALLENGE AND NEW IDEAS

Every leader, not only in museums, should be open to challenge and new ideas. Any leader should be able to articulate their vision in order to enlist supporters (be they members, shareholders, the public or staff) and also be open to new ideas from whatever quarter. Leaders should not think they have a monopoly on good ideas: indeed, the ideal leader welcomes challenge, which brings fresh perspectives on the process of change (see also Chapters 51 and 52, on reflective practice and external voices).

A nurse will have a different opinion about the strengths and weaknesses of a health service from a consultant surgeon. So it is in museums also. The opinions of members of staff will be coloured by their job, their colleagues and whether they have regular and frequent contact with members of the public/users or with the museum's governing body.

There will always be different perspectives. If you work with the public all day every day, your view of the needs of the museum and of the change(s) you think are important could be radically different from someone who works behind the scenes. A museum director will never see the same reaction from users as someone who is on the admissions desk.

Embracing this diversity of opinions and perspectives can only make the museum stronger if they are incorporated into the change process. Ideas about change must take into account differing viewpoints in order to be most effective. Change needs to be embraced by every type and level of staff/volunteers if it is to succeed.

As a museum leader you should not think that it just needs you: you should not shoulder all the burden of the change. You should be *leading* the change, *directing* it, but not *doing* all of it. Creating a Change Working or Implementation Group is a helpful tool to steer your change process and involve many of your staff/volunteers. They can be used to test your ideas, implement pilots, and give feedback about how your ideas could be received by a wide range of the staff. They can also be used as a Task and Finish Group, too, to ensure that no loose ends are left when you come to a milestone at the end of a phase of change.

A highly effective method of incorporating different voices into your change process is to use a diagonal slice of staff/volunteers in the Change Working or Implementation Group. This is effective because a slice ensures all levels of staff/volunteers across different museum roles are included, and therefore ideally all viewpoints should be represented. Crucially, the diagonal element means that the more junior staff will not be present alongside their direct line managers, and so should be able to contribute more readily and be honest about potential impacts or problems. As long as the leader is prepared to listen and adapt, these different perspectives should make the change process stronger, more effective and more successful.

See also:

8   Balancing conflicting priorities
33   Staff/volunteer development and change
34   Champions of change
52   External voice and critical friends

12

EXPLORE AND TEST – THE VALUE OF PILOT PROJECTS

In industrial research and development, where millions of pounds may be needed to develop and introduce a new gizmo, it is a tried and tested approach to pilot at least a prototype. Piloting projects – just trying things out, sometimes on a smaller scale – is a sensible way of museums dipping their change toes in the water.

This is not a popular way of introducing change in museums (though as authors we are not sure why!), but it is an approach used elsewhere in the cultural sector. The Royal Shakespeare Company regularly uses experiments and constant small-scale innovations to help change to happen. They have reflected on the many advantages of undertaking limited but continuous experiments.[1]

- Experiments and pilots are less threatening than major change.
- They can be retracted if the innovation proves problematic.
- Experiments are easier to slow down or speed up than large-scale change.
- They are less expensive than wholesale change.
- Pilots create momentum and stimulus.
- They focus energy and develop confidence.
- Pilots can create quick wins and provide opportunities for celebration.
- Experimentation acknowledges that different parts of an organisation move at a different pace.

Obviously, if the change is large or likely to impact the organisation in a fundamental way, it would not be possible to replicate it completely, but a small aspect of the change could be piloted. An appropriate example could be a new communications strategy (see Chapter 39), but communicating simply about current day-to-day operational news. If you are considering introducing new staff meetings, discussion groups, newsletters pinned onto staff noticeboards or a WhatsApp (or similar) group, then trying these out without a change sword of Damocles hanging over staff/volunteers may be a true test of how effective the system would be during the real change process.

If whatever you chose to test, maybe one or two aspects, does not work, then this will give you an opportunity to correct or amend before going 'live'. Or if it did work well, then once the change process has begun, the staff will be familiar with anything you have piloted, and will feel more comfortable about using it. This could significantly reduce stress during the change as familiarity should help staff to feel safer, if not to provide comfort.

Before embarking on a small-scale change pilot, consider carefully what you want to learn about the effectiveness of the processes and ways of working that you are introducing, and the likely outcomes. Think about a pragmatic approach to collecting sufficient, reliable data about the processes and results that can help you to know whether this is a promising approach (see Chapter 49: Tracking your change journey). Allow sufficient time for evaluation and learning. Do not be tempted to track an unrealistic number of changes that can only be expected to emerge over a longer period.

Some funders offer grants explicitly for these types of shorter pilots (typically up to two years), to explore, test and evaluate a particular new approach that might be rolled out across the organisation more extensively in the future, and are happy to support work that carries a degree of risk.

See also:

28   Embracing risk

Note

1   R. Hewison, J. Holden and S. Jones, *All together: A creative approach to organisational change* (Demos 2010), p. 127.

13

EXPECT CHAOS

> Everything has been turned upside down. It's in confusion, no one knows how to get anything done. . . . Eventually I embraced the chaos. I said if this place is different, I'll be different too.
>
> Dennis Slater, Glenbow Museum[1]

Part 2 has been about preparing for change. But, no matter how well you prepare and subsequently manage your change programme, some things will go wrong, or at least not to plan. There will be an element of chaos. Expecting it and being ready for it are part of good preparation.

Such chaos is well documented during change in museums and other arts organisations: it is normal, and not 'failure'.[2] Indeed, it seems to be a necessary part of change. Change on an organisation-wide scale will be an upheaval for your museum. Your staff/volunteers may be expected to work in radically different ways and, as result, staff may feel under pressure. During a process of change many things are in flux, and there is often confusion around roles and decision-making – who does what and who is responsible – and it is common for staff to feel a deep sense of instability.

> Some staff get anxious, but stability is a fallacy. It's false to ask when it's all going to settle down.
>
> NCAF Grantee-Partner[3]

Human beings can be unpredictable once under pressure. Leaders need to anticipate and be aware of such confusion and anxiety and to provide clarity around roles and responsibilities, otherwise staff will default to pre-change lines of hierarchy, authority and ways of working. Several key staff responding negatively to change or attempting to sabotage it could have a detrimental impact on your whole change process.

> I have no discomfort in admitting that Glenbow often appears to be slightly out of control. This is reputedly a desirable characteristic of new organizations, as it is associated with the creation of unforeseen results, innovation and overall organizational flexibility. It is also associated with some chaos and failure. . . and a certain amount of stress, however, among those staff who prefer more prediction and uniformity.
>
> Robert Janes, *Museums and the Paradox of Change*[4]

In today's world, change is constant, whether planned or not. Organisations need to be able to adapt and be flexible, and to live with uncertainty and constantly changing circumstances with a manageable level of anxiety as the norm. Unanticipated global events over which you have no control, as noted in the Introduction, may have a chaotic and long-term impact on your museum. You must cope in these situations as best you can and it is often difficult, if not impossible, to plan ahead.

Anticipating chaos can therefore be a strength in a museum leader. You will be able to deal with it more effectively and more swiftly if it is anticipated. If it comes round a blind corner to bite you unexpectedly, the results may be catastrophic.

So things can go wrong, the change wagon may lose a wheel or two, but you may not lose sleep over it as it may seem inevitable to you. You may think that it will not materially affect the outcome. However, it may delay the change process being completed and may damage some of your plans, or affect the motivation of some of your key staff and allies. Those who are not wholeheartedly supporting the change process could use this moment to sabotage your change, as the chaos may mean you take your eye off the ball for a split second.

So anticipation and clarity about short- and long-term aims, and about roles and decision-making criteria, are key to the chaos not overwhelming the organisation.

See also:

19 Values, behaviours and cultural change
29 Don't be afraid to report problems or 'failure'
30 Fear of change
31 Countering resistance to change
32 Supporting staff and volunteers during change

Notes

1 Quoted in R.R. Janes, *Museums and the paradox of change: A case study in urgent adaptation* (third edition, Routledge 2013), p. 139.
2 S. Lee and K. Gean, *The Engagement Revolution: A study of strategic organizational transformation in 10 California arts nonprofits* (James Irvine Foundation 2017), p. 38; G. Anderson, 'Reflections on organizational transformation in the twenty-first century', in R.R. Janes, *Museums and the paradox of change: A case study in urgent adaptation* (third edition, Routledge 2013), p. 201.
3 Quoted in S. Lee and K. Gean, *The Engagement Revolution: A study of strategic organizational transformation in 10 California arts nonprofits* (James Irvine Foundation 2017), p. 38.
4 R.R. Janes, *Museums and the paradox of change: A case study in urgent adaptation* (third edition, Routledge 2013), p. 164.

PART 3
Leading change

Effective leadership of a change programme is self-evidently crucial to its success, and this part looks at the qualities of a good change leader and the role of a governing body. This includes building trust in both the leader and the change process itself, embracing risk and not being afraid to make mistakes. Sustaining momentum over a long period is not easy, and Chapter 21 also includes guidance on sustaining change in times of crisis.

But leaders cannot achieve success on their own – a key thread running through this book is that change is everyone's job and responsibility. An effective change programme involves staff, volunteers, communities and stakeholders in decision-making and management. So Part 3 also looks at who and what can support and assist the leader in achieving successful change, through devolved and distributed leadership and reappraisal of values and behaviours.

14

WHAT MAKES A GOOD
CHANGE LEADER?

If the support for change does not start and stop with the chief executive officer or the executive director, then change will not happen.

Robert Janes, *Museums and the Paradox of Change*[1]

A leader of organisational change needs five key characteristics:

- Determination.
- Flexibility.
- Political antennae.
- Empathy/sensitivity.
- Complete belief in the changes they are about to deliver.

In addition, a thick skin is hugely helpful. These qualities apply to directors, chairs of governing bodies, or any other types of leader.

Determination

If the leader in question has initiated and framed the change, then they will believe in it and this will help to make them a more credible change leader. It also underlines their authority, as they are less likely to give way or agree to unsuitable concessions if challenged. Initially, a change leader will need this in order to get their change programme adopted by the museum's governing body (assuming it is a significant enough process to need policy approval). When in the implementation phase, demonstrating your determination is important to show your single-minded pursuit of the change, especially if you expect to face opposition from the staff at this point.

But **flexibility** is also important as the best laid plans may, through no fault of the leader, go awry. Taking opportunities that arise to achieve your goals is a crucial skill for any leader, but in change it can offer unexpected or surprising avenues towards success. As the world will continue turning during your implementation, you will need to adapt and take account of external events which may impact on your change programme. Flexibility also includes being open to alternative ideas and approaches, which may come from any source – staff, volunteers, governing body or community partners (see Chapter 11). For leadership in times of crisis, and sustaining change, see Chapter 21.

Political antennae are crucial for any leader, but particularly one who is leading change. Politics in this case are not necessarily the party politics of central or local government but the politics of power, so are applicable in whatever type of organisation (or even sector) you operate. These are part of the sensitivity needed to interpret what you smell blowing in the wind, and so adapt or alter your course. Be fleet of foot to be able to take advantage of these opportunities.

Empathy/sensitivity

There are several different types of sensitivity required. Empathy and sensitivity to the responses of staff and volunteers are crucial, not only towards those who worry about losing their jobs as a result of the change, but because human beings are creatures of habit: they fear change as an upheaval to their lives and work, and a threat to their equilibrium. So demonstrating your empathy with the reactions of staff and volunteers will be important for the success of the change programme – for this, you need to be able to listen effectively, both to what is said and not said, and to be aware of body language, which can often be more revealing than words. Otherwise, you risk losing potential allies by reacting in an unexpected way. You need to trust your instincts to allow your empathy to operate effectively. Instincts are important when you are under pressure and making decisions quickly, so in the hot-house of a change programme you need to be sure what and who you can trust. Doing so will help you to clarify exactly what your instincts are telling you.

Belief

Self-confidence is important for any leader at any time, but in leading and championing change it is vital. The leader(s) must be able to demonstrate belief in the change. It is not sufficient to simply believe in the change itself, but to have credibility you must be seen to be confident and believe in what you are doing. If the change is your initiative, or if you have been given the responsibility to deliver it, then you must be seen to have faith in it yourself or you cannot expect the staff and volunteers to do so.

Leaders should actively champion the change: and this applies not just to the director but to members of the governing body and senior managers; otherwise they can be a block to change. All staff, funders and stakeholders must recognise leaders' commitment to change. Active championing means constantly reinforcing the message about change, at every opportunity – not just once, at an all-staff meeting, but at every meeting, so that no one can be in any doubt about what is happening.

All leaders who are successful at change have a strong focus on the matter in hand, and are not easily distracted or waylaid by other events or priorities. Their determination is crucial to successful change leadership.

Having a **thick skin** will prove useful for the leader to preserve their sanity. The reaction from frightened staff can easily be focused on one person, but the leader must be able to step aside and recognise that, usually, it is not aimed at them as an individual but is symptomatic of the uncertainty and fear in the minds of their staff.

But not all leaders are good at change; some are better at operational leadership, practical or strategic considerations, with the leading of change not being their strength. If you are placed in a position of having to lead change – or if you choose to put yourself there – then it is wise to know your capabilities, strengths and weaknesses in order to be effective. You may find it useful to source some training and especially mentoring from experienced change leaders, both inside and outside the museum sector, who will help develop and support you and give you practical tips (on mentoring, see Chapter 54).

See also:

21   How to sustain change
22   Change of director during the change process
23   Distributed leadership and sharing decision-making
28   Embracing risk
29   Don't be afraid to report problems or 'failure'

Note

1   R.R. Janes, *Museums and the paradox of change: A case study in urgent adaptation* (third edition, Routledge 2013), p. 84.

15

GOVERNANCE AND CHANGE

To survive, all museums must adapt and bend in the wind to ensure they can remain relevant to the public, who in many cases own the collections, sites and buildings. If history and museums are to help people understand the past, cope with their present and be strong enough to face their future, museums must be relevant and tell their stories in a way that the public can engage with and understand. Periodically, therefore, museums need to reinvent themselves, just as leading brands in the consumer world relaunch and refresh their image and products.

If the change has been initiated by the board,[1] it is likely that the board members will already have recognised that some fundamental rethinking is required to build a resilient museum. But if the change has been introduced from an external source, by another person or organisation – for example, a new director or a government body – then the board themselves may have to take an active part in the change process and change themselves too.

Developing and changing the board

First of all, ensure that your board is discussing the right things in the right way. Some boards tend to focus on day-to-day matters, and the meetings might even be a bit unstructured – this is often the case in small, local museums, which are largely volunteer-run, and maybe do not have a large pool of experienced potential board members from which to draw. It is important that the board pays most of its attention to more strategic issues that are its responsibility – such as the longer-term strategic direction of the museum – and to structure the meetings accordingly. In this way, the board will control the direction of change.

If the museum is changing the emphasis of its public programme – exhibitions, events, learning and family programmes – then the outlook of the board and their skills will probably need to be transformed too in order for the change to be implemented. If an independent museum, for example, was initially created in the late twentieth century (as many industrial archaeology museums in the UK were from the late 1970s to 1990s), then the board is likely to be full of experts in the subject matter, site and collections of that museum. When museums are bumping along the bottom and worried they may go bankrupt, the board is likely to be peopled by financial and legal experts, as many were in the early years of the twenty-first century. Of course, these skills are needed on any governing body to some extent, but not to the exclusion of those who have a curatorial or learning background, experience of running a visitor attraction, or developing trading and income streams.

Many boards still recruit from among people the existing trustees know personally; in these circumstances, they always get more of the same. Some feel uncertain about going outside their comfort zone, and open recruitment is still often seen as risky. However, if the change process needs to introduce new skills and a new outlook onto the board, then open recruitment is often the most effective way of reaching new people. This process should include a formal skills audit to assess exactly what knowledge, skills and experience the board needs to have across all its members, and a formal assessment of the candidates – just like a job interview. Open recruitment is also a perfect opportunity for the museum to generate some positive publicity for itself: for local media, a museum shifting emphasis, wanting to engage more with its public and seeking fresh blood to help them to do so, is a terrific news story. This, in turn, may introduce potential new audiences to the museum.

Elsewhere we explore broadening involvement in creating and implementing change and in developing the museum (see Chapters 8, 24 and 25). A change in the emphasis of how the museum functions, for example to a more democratic and 'liberal' outlook with participation and wider community connections, may mean a psychological shift for many boards. The concept of the participatory museum may be a new one to a trustee from a more traditional background; the majority of museum visitors (and consumers of culture in general), certainly in the UK and much of Europe, are still middle class, middle aged and well educated. Consequently, if broadening the audience and involving them directly in the work of the museum is a new development, then experience of this way of working must be represented on the board to guide and oversee the change, and reassure more reluctant board members.

However, in these cases, boards are often slower to play an active leadership role, and might even show resistance, especially where a change measurably affects the organisation's core or traditional programming, and when it starts to affect its business model. An evaluation of change at ten museums and arts organisations in California noted that such cases inspired the most fraught discussions between staff and board, and sometimes resulted in the organisation having to slow down or scale back its ambitions. This was particularly true where some long-serving board members regarded engagement as anathema to artistic quality. Often, committed staff wanted such work to progress more quickly, while a board had concerns about whether changes to the traditional programming might alienate the current audience and threaten the organisation's financial base (see Chapter 8 on conflicting priorities). A leader sometimes ends up being a mediator between staff and the board, but if the leader is not actively championing the work, the board's resistance or slowing down the change can demoralise staff.[2]

The solution to this is to provide opportunities for training, ongoing involvement – such as attending meetings with community partners or participating in programming – and evaluation of their involvement for members of boards. Essentially this creates champions of the change on the board, whose role is to help advocate the work with other trustees, internally across the museum, and externally with funders, politicians and others.[3]

The lesson is that a change programme potentially affects everyone: the board, too, may need to change and must be open to change. It is essential, therefore, that members are prepared to challenge others on the board and the director, and that part of the skills audit and recruitment process for board members includes the ability and willingness to challenge the status quo in a positive and constructive way.

Support for leaders and staff

Staff and volunteers who may be nervous about fundamental change or upheaval could be comforted by the involvement of the board, whether as leaders or as participants. If they understand that they themselves are not being singled out, then they are likely to be more reassured than otherwise. It is important, therefore, that all trustees recognise their supportive role here and know what to say, and what not to say, if staff approach them about their own concerns (see also Chapter 39).

Fundamental changes which impact on policy will require the governing body to approve them. If the museum is a charity, then the charitable objects which govern and specify what the museum can do need to be updated whenever a significant shift occurs to the mission and activities of the museum. Other strategic changes could include alterations to staffing, admission charges policy or structure, or to programming, collecting and display policies. So the board has an active role to play both as a leader and as advisers, in addition to using their skills and knowledge in certain professional or technical areas. Obviously, the change programme, if it introduces the above elements, will need board approval and they should also agree on an implementation timescale, especially if there are resource implications.

The director, however, as the day-to-day leader of the museum, will also need support throughout this process. The day job – ensuring the museum keeps operating effectively – is a challenge during any major project, but with staff not firing on all cylinders all the time, and concern and perhaps fear within the organisation, the director needs to not only keep the museum and its programmes going but continue to deliver the change programme too. Personal and practical support for them is therefore important, and the board must understand its duty of care as an employer. An external mentor or change coach may be helpful here, even if the director has a substantial network themselves (see Chapter 54). Boards should not assume that a director will be comfortable and be able to sleep at night when the going gets sticky, so they need to recognise their responsibilities and be active as a caring employer.

Leading change

In many chapters of this book, the authors have assumed that the director is either the initiator of change or is delivering it with enthusiasm and belief. However, on occasion it is possible that this is not the case, and that the director also needs to be changed. If this is so, then the board must be a key player in the development and delivery of the change.

In this situation, in our experience, there may (or should) be two or three on the board who have particular experience and knowledge of change at this level. They should be given a clear mandate to lead the board's work in this area, with delegated powers to keep the process moving forward. Milestones must be agreed on for this group to report back to the board, and everyone should be kept up to date in between, without overwhelming one and all in endless email threads.

The board will also have a vital role to play if change is being imposed from external sources, for example, from a major revenue funder or a government agency. Sadly, there are recent examples in Europe of political appointments and interference in major museums around appointments of chief executives because of their affiliations to a political party/government (see Chapter 44). This has resulted in inexperienced directors who are incapable of leading the change they have been appointed to achieve, with consequent spectacular failures, or introducing change which was not needed.

Museums are complicated animals, and those which sit within a commercial organisation, as some museums in the UK do, often have chief executives imposed who do not have a heritage background or any understanding of the sector. Their ability to lead is severely compromised and their judgement, when not informed by the complexities of the professional organisation, can cause knee-jerk reactions in responding to opportunities.

In these situations, the main board is likely to have minimal understanding of the heritage sector, so access to the board is important for the leader of the museum itself, who is likely to have a background in museum work, unlike the chief executive. There may be a committee or similar to whom the museum director reports. If the main company/charity is run more commercially, it may be that the museum business is considered at best window dressing, or at worst not good value for money. In this relationship, the director must make it a priority to educate the 'museum committee' about what being a museum actually means in both the world and in the context of the main company or charity. If you need to push on with a change programme, it is vital that your board/committee understands why this is necessary and does not dismiss your ideas as fiddling round the edges. This is always a challenge and this relationship does not always work: it requires determination and sensitivity, and sometimes the solution is to call on respected external voices to whom the board will listen (see Chapter 52).

The role of the governing body during change is one of both leadership and participatory support. They must maintain their distance from the director and executive staff, but must also be seen to be mentoring where necessary and monitoring progress. It is often a fine balance, but where the board can find that balance, the museum can fly.

See also:

8   Balancing conflicting priorities
18 Revisiting the mission
19 Values, behaviours and cultural change
22 Change of director during change process

Notes

1   In this chapter the governing body is called 'the board' even though they may not be trustees of an independent charity. Whatever their name, they are in a position of governance and leadership of the organisation, even if the museum is not an independent charity.
2   S. Lee and K. Gean, *The Engagement Revolution: A study of strategic organizational transformation in 10 California arts nonprofits* (James Irvine Foundation 2017), pp. 48–49.
3   P. Bienkowski, *No longer us and them: How to change into a participatory museum and gallery – Learning from the Our Museum programme* (Paul Hamlyn Foundation 2016), p. 22.

16

FUNDING AND RESOURCING CHANGE

Change takes time and it needs to be funded adequately. But there are two distinct issues here: one is funding and resourcing the change process itself; the other is funding and resourcing the running of the transformed museum in a manner that can be sustained. While both ultimately depend on the four standard sources of museum funding – revenue streams (sometimes public), earned income, project grants and donations (the balance between them depending on the museum's constitution) – the approaches vary.

Resourcing the change process

Change is a process – a series of activities by a group of people over time, which has resource implications. At the very least, if you are focused on a change programme, it means you are not doing something else.

There are obvious financial implications in changing or adjusting people's jobs, even temporarily during the change process, and these costs must be identified as part of the preparation for change, before the finance is needed. Physical space and costs for specific meetings, away days, confidential sessions or additional meetings of the board must also be funded. The time taken in discussions, formal and informal consultations and in reflection by the leadership must all be anticipated. You may wish to test some changes on a small scale, and these will need to be resourced (see Chapter 12: Explore and test).

All of these activities and mechanisms should be identified beforehand, costed and incorporated into the business plan. Unless they are costed and in the business plan, there is a real danger that they will not happen, as the 'day job' will take over, and the change will not progress. Increasingly, there are project grants available for museums to kick-start a change process and to trial different approaches, learning what works and what doesn't in their particular environment. If you don't have a project grant to resource the change process, then you will have to find the funds from elsewhere in your core budget, and that might mean making difficult decisions about which museum activities not to do while you are focusing on change. If some of those activities are revenue streams, then you will have to take into account reduced income during the change process.

Resourcing sustainable change

It is often the case that change is stimulated by the stark realisation that the traditional way of doing things can no longer be funded and resourced sustainably. You may be facing a financial deficit. In those instances, savings have to be found from doing things differently, sometimes with fewer people organised in a different way, with less money. But it can be difficult to cut museum overhead costs without a negative impact on the collections and exhibition spaces.

Alternatively, new income streams have to be identified, which will also have an impact on what the museum offers, to whom, and on which activities it might levy a charge. Governing bodies and directors are understandably sometimes more concerned about revenue streams than about innovative ways of working. In parallel to this, staff may be more committed to new participatory ways of working as innovation to them may be more interesting than worrying about income. Tensions can arise when boards worry about the financial implications of changes, particularly where they might alienate the current audience and threaten the financial base. In the USA, some progressive museums and arts organisations are cultivating sources of individual giving from new donors whose values align with their changed mission and approach, premised on a commitment to inclusivity, connection and community engagement, rather than the exclusivity and privilege of the traditional trustee-donor, subscriber or member (see Chapter 8: Balancing conflicting priorities).[1]

The essence of the business planning process is to prioritise the activities that will fulfil the museum's mission, and to fund and schedule them. Whatever changes you have made should be embedded into business as usual, so the costs get subsumed into the core budgets of the museum and the new activities are not regarded as a 'nice extra' that is optional. This is especially true of changes to outreach or participatory work that may have become fundamental to delivering corporate aims.

For example, Amgueddfa Cymru-National Museum Wales used changes to its approach to volunteering as a catalyst for wider organisational change, broadening the diversity of volunteers, addressing the needs of the volunteers and not just those of the museum, and involving volunteers in decision-making.[2] In terms of costs and income to sustain this changed way of working, they made a distinction between community volunteering with partners such as homeless charities, which was free, and corporate volunteering, where companies that volunteer as a team-building opportunity were subject to a charge that covered the museum's costs. Any underspend was reinvested in the volunteer programme to make it sustainable. In this way, attracting paying groups to the programme can be seen as a sustainable funding model delivering strategic aims, where similar services are charged to some, for example, corporate customers, so that other participants can benefit at subsidised, low or zero costs.

Sometimes, too, strategic partnerships are ways of sharing costs and resources to sustain a new way of working (see Chapter 25 on community partnerships and change). All partners have resources and assets, and an effective partnership creates a resource pool that every partner can draw on. Museums have successfully partnered with libraries, schools, churches and other cultural institutions, to cooperate and share resources and spaces rather than compete.[3] Such sharing of resources and costs among a number of museum partners in particular geographical areas has been tried successfully, and may become more popular and widespread as a way of creating sustainable, resilient museums (see Chapter 21 on sustaining change).

Emotional resources

There is also an emotional cost to every aspect of change. Change, particularly from the leader's point of view, can be emotionally taxing as you may feel constantly 'on parade'. You will need relentless supplies of energy, as you will expend it ensuring the programme moves at the speed you desire and doesn't stall. You will have to keep everyone else going when they flag, and head off opposition or sabotage to protect the change. Maintaining your own reserves of determination is crucial; recognise that you need allies to help you do this (see Chapter 23: Distributed leadership and sharing decision-making).

As the leader, you will not be able to maintain your usual work routine, as the emphasis of your day job will inevitably change. Routine is comforting in times of stress or crisis, but leading change will be an upheaval in your work life. This may appear to be a very obvious thing to point out, but many are surprised by the impact of leading a change programme on themselves. This alone takes energy to process, but must not distract you from leadership.

You will need to take time out of the day job, to create the head space to consider and reflect on progress, to solve problems and consider the next steps. This means you may not be available for other tasks and not so visible and accessible to staff, who will have their own emotional reactions to change (see Chapter 42 on acknowledging emotions). Be aware of the impact on their morale of such absence – there needs to be a balance between your need to think things through in tranquillity, and their need for your support through a confusing time, especially if they feel that change is being done to them. Sustaining the emotional resources of your staff and volunteers is crucial to the success of the change programme (see Chapters 32 and 35 on how to support staff).

See also:

8   Balancing conflicting priorities
21   How to sustain change
23   Distributed leadership and sharing decision-making

Notes

1 S. Lee and K. Gean, *The Engagement Revolution: A study of strategic organizational transformation in 10 California arts nonprofits* (James Irvine Foundation 2017).

2 P. Bienkowski, *No longer us and them: How to change into a participatory museum and gallery – Learning from the Our Museum programme* (Paul Hamlyn Foundation 2016), p. 29.

3 See, e.g. M. Schwarzer, 'No heroes: Revisiting the museum leadership crisis', in R.R. Janes, *Museums and the paradox of change: A case study in urgent adaptation* (third edition, Routledge 2013), p. 252.

17

STAYING RELEVANT

> For a museum to survive and thrive today, it must be relevant and meaningful for many people from many backgrounds. It must sway to the pulse of the cultural community in which it resides.
>
> Nina Simon[1]

What audiences, communities, funders and other stakeholders demand of museums is constantly changing. Museums are facing particular pressure to tell more diverse stories and respond to the histories of colonialism and slavery. 'Relevance' is not static. All museums should be relevant to their public in order to use their collections to inspire, entertain, educate and generally enhance the quality of life. If museums are not relevant to their audiences, communities and stakeholders, they cannot do this.[2]

Lack of relevance has consequences! The Museum of Vancouver's increasing lack of relevance to its community was reflected in sagging attendance, lack of awareness of the existence of the museum, and problems with funding and donations. In its CEO's words, it was 'heading to an inevitable and certain demise', and required transformative change including a new vision, direction and relevance to the city.[3] A museum that does not recognise its lack of relevance, and does not change to address it, may not be worth preserving.

An effective leader recognises that a museum must continually evolve in order to stay relevant. One of the reasons why organisational change seems never to stop is that the external environment is constantly changing, so the museum must continuously adapt to changing funding streams, stakeholder expectations and unexpected crises. The change leader's job is to build a culture that thrives on innovation and continuous adaptation and improvement.

There are five tried and tested ways for a museum – or any other organisation – to stay relevant. They are all covered in different parts of this book, because they are not separate from change but an integral part of it.

- Encourage innovation and new ideas, and be open to challenges to traditional ways of doing things (see Chapter 11).
- Provide training and resources: change creates the need for people to learn and develop (see Chapter 32).
- Promote cross-functional teams to ensure cross-fertilisation of ideas across different museum roles (see Chapter 40).
- Celebrate mistakes: you will learn from them and get better (see Chapter 29).
- Most importantly, include external perspectives in your change programme, through involving stakeholders, communities and critical friends (see Chapters 24, 25 and 52). Their viewpoints will help keep you grounded in what is relevant to them and to wider society.

See also:

18 Revisiting the mission
19 Values, behaviours and cultural change
24 Involving stakeholders in the change process
25 Community partnerships and change

Notes

1 Quoted in G. Dunn, 'How Nina Simon reinvented Santa Cruz art', *Good Times* (Santa Cruz), 4 June 2019, goodtimes.sc/cover-stories/nina-simon-reinvented-art-santa-cruz/.
2 N. Simon, *The art of relevance* (Museum 2.0 2016).
3 N. Noble, 'Museum of Vancouver – A transformation in progress', in R.R. Janes, *Museums and the paradox of change: A case study in urgent adaptation* (third edition, Routledge 2013), p. 227.

18

REVISITING THE MISSION

A new vision for an organisation may come about as a result of new leadership or – in a chicken and egg way – may be the stimulus for the new mission. Likely reasons for museums reassessing their mission include a change in funding priorities from an external source (e.g. government), public opinion changing about the core story of the museum (e.g. the slave trade) or a capital project which brings investment and requires new ways of working as a result.[1] All these reasons will demand organisational change.

It is usually external pressures which dictate that a museum needs to change. Some of these pressures are financial, some political and some are a result of natural disasters (flood, storm, fire or infection). These pressures may cause a change of leadership: a new director and/or chair. These changes themselves may be a result of the leadership realising that a shift in the museum's mission and/or activities was required.

So whether the change is the outcome or the cause of a new mission, it is pragmatic for the leadership of the museum to ensure that the whole organisation can contribute to the new mantra. Everyone connected to the museum must 'buy into' the change if it is to be successful.

Throughout this book, involving staff and volunteers is recommended to ensure that change is positive and inclusive. But if the mission is being reassessed, then the differing viewpoints of staff and volunteers, with their many different roles, are absolutely crucial if the mission is to be valid. The whole organisation needs to sign up to the new mission, as it is not simply the preserve of the board and the senior leadership team.

An effective way of testing your current mission is to examine how it reflects or links to your founding stories: the collection and stories told about it when your museum first opened. Depending on how old your museum is, some of these stories may need telling in a radically different way, for example, in industrial museums where the industry itself has disappeared, rural museums where the traditional ways of living and working have been forgotten or where younger generations do not understand historical facts as older people did, for example, those museums which concentrate on the Second World War. New display techniques and interpretation may also allow complex stories to be told differently, perhaps through digital media, to reach new audiences.

For example, the Museum of East Anglian Life in the UK, originally founded to save the farming heritage of East Anglia, developed a new strategic focus on food, exploring the issues and challenges of the past, present and future, which gave it a new sense of purpose and relevance to modern audiences. Revisiting their mission led to a realisation that their collections could be used to tell stories in a different and more relevant way (see end of Chapter 8 for their consultative process).

Such exercises give a museum a clearer understanding of its mission today and whether its historic mission needs updating and/or changing. This work then leads on to reassessing the values of the organisation, another key step in achieving cultural change (Chapter 19).

See also:

7   What is your stimulus for change?
17   Staying relevant
19   Values, behaviours and cultural change

Note

1   Though, in reality, the museum may adjust its mission in order to attract the funding.

19

VALUES, BEHAVIOURS AND CULTURAL CHANGE

Organisational values are the core principles which guide the behaviours of everyone in the museum, in whatever circumstances. They are a clear statement about the aspirations of the museum. Having clear values helps ensure that everyone is working towards the same goals. They inspire staff's best efforts and also constrain their actions. Strong, clearly articulated values should be a reflection of the sort of museum you want to be and your aspirations for appropriate workplace behaviour. They play an important role in building a positive culture in your organisation. Their purpose is as an ideal, a 'guiding star' by which staff, volunteers and the governing body can align their individual contributions with the overall direction of the organisation.[1]

Many museums now have clearly articulated statements of values, but whether you do or not, they must reflect reality and be in step with your vision and mission. Typical museum values include trust, integrity, respect for the individual, dialogue and debate, promotion of intercultural understanding, community engagement, creativity and generosity.

Well-articulated museum values:

- guide the behaviour of staff, volunteers and the governing body, as well as strategic and operational decisions
- inform and improve the museum's operations and culture
- demonstrate integrity and accountability to external stakeholders
- reduce the risk of inappropriate behaviour.

Changing your mission and values may be a result of a new way of working, or they may be the stimulus for a new way of working. On the one hand, your mission and values must change so that they support, illustrate and are relevant for the new style of organisation, but, on the other hand, the change programme may be introduced and designed as a result of re-examining your mission and values first, which will affect how you do things.

Values signify that the organisation has, or seeks, harmony. They should be discussed, explored and shaped jointly as an organisation. The aim should be to reach consensus on shared values, rather than imposing them on a sceptical work-force. The process should involve a broad cross-section of staff and volunteers, the governing body and ideally community partners too, giving everyone an opportunity to talk about wide-ranging and fundamental topics in a safe setting. This may be seen as an irrelevant distraction – and not everyone is comfortable talking about values – but once you begin to discuss them, even the most sceptical staff member should see their importance.

The process typically involves:

- in-depth discussions with the governing body, leaders and senior managers
- focus groups with staff, volunteers and community partners
- listening to all their views about what the museum stands for now, and what value shifts it wants to make in the future
- preparing a draft statement of values, based on what staff and stakeholders tell you
- working collaboratively to refine and finalise the values, and develop an implementation and communication strategy.

It is also useful for individual staff members and volunteers to think about and understand their own core values and how they match those of the organisation. Research has revealed a direct link between finding a synergy, or a lack of it, between personal, professional and organisational values, and maintaining a positive and constructive sense of worth as a museum professional. Most negative emotions surface when values are misaligned or incompatible.[2] Involving all staff in the exploration of shared values helps mitigate this.

Values both reflect and stimulate cultural change. The culture of an organisation is best defined as 'the way we do things here'. Much of organisational culture is an unconscious set of assumptions and behaviours. Changing an organisation's culture is difficult, because it comprises an interlocking set of these assumptions and behaviours, alongside values, processes, attitudes and working practices. These elements tend to reinforce each other, making it difficult to change the overall culture.

Things can go wrong if too much coercion is used to force a culture change. Developing a shared vision, mission and values is often an important first step, combined with developing staff and volunteers (see Chapter 33). Focusing on being outward-looking, welcoming and valuing all visitors, whatever their needs, and tolerating demands from the public, are just a few of the sensitive areas for discussion. These could lead to a step change in behaviour generally, which is a key stage in changing the overall culture of an organisation.

Do not expect everyone and everything to change immediately. The best results often come from working with allies and champions of change, who are already natural supporters of a different way of working, to model the new behaviour and culture (see Chapter 34). If these allies and champions reflect a cross-section of your museum, then over time their behaviour will affect that of others. Culture change is a process – usually a long one – not a single event.

The authors have both worked through significant shifts in the culture of museums, which have moved from quite formal, traditional organisations where everyone who was a professional curator, for example, was addressed by their surname and handle, to ones where everyone, even the director, is addressed by all staff by their first name. This, of course, mirrors social changes, primarily in the western world, and many of the shifts in museums have also done so. Museums have moved, sometimes far too slowly, to being more open to new ideas and reflecting the world around them.

See also:

17   Staying relevant
18   Revisiting the mission
21   How to sustain change
55   Fixing the lessons of change in organisational memory

Notes

1   D. Fleming, 'The essence of the museum: Mission, values, vision', in C. McCarthy (ed.), *Museum practice* (Wiley Blackwell 2015), pp. 3–25; R. Hewison, J. Holden and S. Jones, *All together: A creative approach to organisational change* (Demos 2010), p. 48.
2   N. Morse and M. McCann, *Becoming a change-maker in museums: Experiences, opportunities and challenges: Reflections on the Museums Association's Transformers Workforce Development Initiative* (University of Leicester 2019), p. 16.

20

BUILDING TRUST

Changing things depends on creating confidence and trust.
Robert Hewison, John Holden and Samuel Jones, *All Together*[1]

Trust enables people to work together more effectively. Trust must be earned, it cannot be bought or bottled, and it cannot be prized too highly.

If you are the leader of a museum, or even of the change programme itself, then you may be viewed with suspicion by those who are against some or all aspects of the change or who are openly opponents of it. Asking your staff and volunteers, whatever your role, to trust you is a pointless exercise, as naturally, unless you know someone extremely well and they are close friends, your audience will automatically be sceptical.

Museum professionals, in the authors' experience, are naturally cynical and are inclined to be suspicious of leaders and managers who want to change things. As a first step, be visible in your museum sites. If staff see you regularly 'on the shop floor', it helps them to start seeing you as a human being whom they can consider trusting, not someone who is holed up in an office and always in a meeting (see Chapter 35).

Meanwhile, accept mistrust as the normal state of affairs with most or all of your staff and volunteers, and you will be on the path of building trust. To earn their trust, you must do six things:

- Never lose sight of the end goal of the change process.
- Be honest, however painful for you or them this might be.

- If events or new information cause you to change what you need to do, be open about this and explain your reasons; transparency helps to create a feeling of shared ownership.
- Actively listen to staff and volunteers, and ensure everyone has the chance for their voice to be heard, ask questions, get answers and voice concerns.
- Deliver what you promise: if you can't ensure it will happen, don't promise.
- Practise what you preach and don't have double standards; if you encourage people to work in teams, then collaborate yourself across teams and functions.

Trust takes time to build. You can't hurry it, but must give it space and time.

See also:

30 Fear of change
31 Countering resistance to change
35 Keeping up morale during change
40 Internal networks and collaboration
48 Museum processes as a barrier to change

Note

1 R. Hewison, J. Holden and S. Jones, *All together: A creative approach to organisational change* (Demos 2010), p. 128.

21

HOW TO SUSTAIN CHANGE

> Change is never a one-off event. It is continuous and ubiquitous. Change happens all the time in our organizations, whether we like it, or know about it, or not.
>
> Darren Peacock[1]

What does sustaining organisational change really mean? Is it to sustain the process of change, or is it about sustaining the change itself? Organisations need both those things – in effect, they need both continuity and change. Organisations that stand still are unresponsive to external changes in their environment and the shifting needs of their communities and stakeholders, but organisations that are in a state of constant revolution are chaotic and unstable.

John Holden uses the analogy of riding a bicycle, in which you can only achieve balance through the right amount of momentum.[2] Sustainability is just that: it means embracing both continuity and change, balance and momentum, at the same time, and getting the organisation to the point where it can pursue its mission efficiently and effectively over a long period of time, but is also able to adapt and respond quickly and easily to any challenges and crises.

Crucially, sustaining change is the polar opposite of one–off projects or 'tick box' exercises with different groups (see Chapter 37). It affects the whole organisation over a long period. Sustaining momentum and the support of staff during this long process of change is not easy, and in every type of organisation, in any sector, the success rate for sustaining successful change is lower than 30 per cent (see Part 5).

The leader's role in sustaining change

Everyone involved with change, in whatever way, must sustain themselves, but the leader(s) must also sustain the process. Belief and determination are essential, as outlined in Chapter 14, but the energy to keep the momentum of change must be provided by the director. Change is not one event or one project, but a continuing process, probably over years, and it may have distinct phases.

Pausing between phases may give you time to recharge your energy – and to embed the changes into the 'new normal' working of the museum – but it could also cause the change process to lose its impetus. Sustaining any major event, be it a climb up a steep hill or a change programme, can be assisted by the end result enticing participants onwards and upwards. In this case, what could support and sustain the process would be the vision of the transformed organisation that will result from the changes.

Over a long period, maybe two or three years, it would be easy for staff to lose sight of this destination. You, however, as the leader, must keep your focus in order to sustain the staff and ensure safe arrival. Your staff may become weary of hearing of the sunny uplands of their future, especially if they are not enthusiastic supporters of your changes, so you must ensure you never lose focus on the 'Why?' (see Chapters 6 and 10).

But as the change leader, whether director or chair, you must also build in energy boosts for yourself. Taking time off, especially at weekends; having a clear dividing line between work and your private life; keeping up with family, friends and spending time with pets or outside with nature are key to keeping your equilibrium and motivation. An obviously tired and weary leader does not inspire confidence, and you yourself would be the barrier to achieving your change goals. Being selfish on occasion is crucial for you to stay sane and keep your perspective.

Quick fixes or little wins will also help to sustain everyone. There are always small things which can be changed with a bit of determination, a little money or a short burst of energy. If these are popular changes, this not only helps to attract support from those who would prefer to resist but can also help to sustain the change process overall.

Sustaining change in times of crisis

Chapter 14 examined the vital qualities needed for a successful change leader. Times of crisis require very different styles of management from day-to-day museum life, so additional qualities are needed to help the museum to recover from a crisis that has caused the loss of change momentum. Especially in smaller museums, curators are required to develop new leadership skills under intense pressure and often in the public eye. Irrespective of the nature of the crisis, there are key requirements to lead the museum through recovery successfully.

- Be visible.
- Be present.

- Be focused.
- Be honest.
- Ask for help.

Be visible: as the change leader, and particularly if you are the director, then you must be visible in all of your museum sites, especially in the public areas, in addition to keeping in touch with your public-facing staff. MBWA – Management by Walking About – is a well-established management tool, but during a time of stress about change, it is even more important, and you cannot be seen too often. If you are not open to the public, then be visible via video link for as many meetings or briefings as possible. All staff, whatever their job, find comfort in seeing and hearing their leader in times of stress. If you are open, this also signals that you are approachable and will listen if a staff member wants to talk to you.

Be present: demonstrate that you're in this crisis too – 'we're in this together' sort of thing. This is the mental aspect of being visible – especially if you are listening to a staff member during one of your MBWA walkabouts. Active listening is a challenge if you're stressed, but it is vital that any staff or volunteers do not get the impression that your mind is not on what they are saying.

Be focused: there is nothing more important than ensuring your staff/ volunteers and your visitors are safe and your museum is as successful as possible. Pet projects or research trips, however long planned, must not take your focus. You must be seen to be concentrating on the matter in hand, even if you aren't and have operational managers who are responsible day-to-day.

Be honest: if you don't know the answer, then say so. If you are working through challenging times, no one knows all of the answers, so if you are unsure, say so. Predicting what might happen when you do not have sufficient evidence or skills to do so is not recommended. Staff will admire you for your honesty more than if you guess and get it wrong.

Ask for help: any crisis is not the time for heroic leadership. Asking for help is not a sign of weakness. Use your allies, friends and contacts to keep yourself informed by every available means. Use your governing body for support and for specific advice where they have expertise. They will want to be useful, but make sure they do not get in the way of pragmatic action. During the UK's Foot and Mouth outbreak in 2001, all rural museums and countryside sites kept in touch with one another and shared information and tips on what to do and what not to do. Professional associations can assist in coordinating information gathering and disseminating to everyone. During the 2020 Covid-19 pandemic, the Association of Independent Museums and the Museums Association in the UK offered free coaching, mentoring and governance support to their members from senior leaders in the sector; while in the USA the American Alliance of Museums, and museum associations at state level, compiled directories of resources, including leading in times of crisis. So use every available tool you can to ensure you are making well-informed decisions, based on evidence and not reinventing a wheel unnecessarily.

Partnerships for resilience

Setbacks and worries about future sustainability – essentially, struggling to stay open in the face of economic problems – often prompt discussion about partnerships or stronger relationships between museums. In such cases, governing bodies and directors worry about loss of individual identity and autonomy – and the museum's sense of its own history – but sharing staff and resources (such as specialist curators, payroll, human resources, and health and safety) can be a way of creating enhanced resilience, so that what is most important about your museum can survive and thrive.

In the UK, for example, Wessex Museums, a partnership of four museums, was formed in 2016 to apply for funding for joint projects. This, and similar examples such as Cornwall Museums Partnership and Cumbria Museums Consortium, all report success after a period of settling down and getting to know each other.[3] Increased cooperation has led them to be more open minded and ambitious, working together on different projects no single museum could achieve on its own, and sharing skilled staff. One curator spoke of taking courage from the group, as it 'wasn't only you on your own'.

There are key factors about partnerships:

- Partnerships need to be equal – there may be safety in numbers but only if there is also equality.
- Everyone must benefit, not just a few of the partners, but you may all need different things; if so, can this partnership provide them?
- Believe in what you are doing or don't join in; for example, when Wessex Museums was forming, one of the potential partners decided it was not for them.
- Make sure it is the right thing for *your* organisation – not just a short-term lifeline. It needs to be longer term for the full benefits to be felt. Does this opportunity fit your 'Why?' (See Chapter 10.)
- Critical mass can be helpful but does everyone *actually* need it?
- Be open minded about where the partnership may take your museum and do not instantly dismiss off-the-wall ideas.

Partnerships are not about loss of an individual museum's identity, but about agreeing to share specific resources and activities to enable all the partners to sustain what is unique about what their own organisation has to offer.

See also:

Notes

1 D. Peacock, 'Complexity, conversation and change: Learning how museum organizations change', in R.R. Janes, *Museums and the paradox of change: A case study in urgent adaptation* (third edition, Routledge 2013), p. 237.
2 J. Holden, 'Thinking about change', extract from *Our Museum* keynote presentation (2015), ourmuseum.org.uk/thinking-about-change/.
3 *Wessex Museums: Our brand story* (Wessex Museums 2019); *Impact Report 2019/2020* (Cornwall Museums Partnership 2020); cumbriamuseums.org.uk.

22

CHANGE OF DIRECTOR DURING CHANGE PROCESS

Reflecting on ten years of change at Glenbow Museum under three different directors, Robert Janes commented:

> [T]here is the disturbing discontinuity stemming from multiple CEOs. Each comes with his or her own aspirations, anxieties and foibles, and the staff must continuously adapt to these. This 10-year revolving courtship at the most senior level has undoubtedly had a serious impact on staff morale and productivity.[1]

If the director leaves the organisation during the change programme, it can disturb the process and impede progress, unless the outgoing director was a block to change and the departure was intended to accelerate it. In most or all cases, there will be an interim leader(s) in place during the ensuing recruitment.

Depending on whether the departure was wished for, lamented or anticipated, the task of maintaining the change momentum will be different. It will depend on who that interim leader is and what impact they may make upon the programme, if any at all.

The authors have both been acting directors themselves and there are often many and varied expectations of such a person, even if the organisation is not in the midst of a change programme. Every staff member will have their own view of what should or should not happen. Everyone's expectations will be high, whether they are opponents or supporters of the changes.

Interim leaders need their power and responsibilities to be defined clearly, and these are likely to be more limited than for a permanent directorial appointment. As a consequence, the momentum of the change may be slowed down, but it is unlikely to be stopped altogether unless the departed director has been discredited.

Opponents of the change programme may take this opportunity to step up their sabotage and, once the new director takes up their post, there will be a slow-down again, so be on your guard for this. The existing senior staff will need to give the new director an inside track on personalities who are opposing the changes. Assuming the new director will take control and lead the change programme, once they have done so with the help of the interim(s), then the momentum can build up once again with the new leader firmly in control.

Table 22.1 lists the common problems and possible solutions regarding sustaining the change process in three different situations: outgoing directors, interim directors and new directors.

TABLE 22.1 Sustaining change with outgoing, interim and new directors

Outgoing directors

Problems	Possible solutions
Directors keep a tight grip on overseeing the change process. There is lack of delegation and staff buy-in.	Governing bodies and champions ideally get engaged in the change process in the first place. Ensure that the recruitment process for the new director emphasises the change management skills required and the direction of travel.
When they leave, no one knows what is happening, or what the organisation is committed to. All impetus is lost.	Outgoing directors should involve all staff in the process. A change process only owned by the director has little chance of succeeding.
Some directors leave just before a financial crisis occurs that threatens sustainability.	Often, the best way of dealing with this is for the governing body to appoint an interim director with a remit to institute a comprehensive business review of the organisation. In this situation, governance structures also need addressing. Even under these circumstances, conversations about why the organisation exists, and what the priorities are can lead to positive change.

Interim directors

Problems	Possible solutions
Interim directors are often chosen specifically to 'hold the fort' and not instigate any more change.	Governing bodies and champions have all the responsibility here: if they are committed to a process of change, then they need to see it through with an interim or new director, rather than play it safe or become risk averse.

Problems	Possible solutions
They are often (though not always) internally appointed, as a 'safe pair of hands'. As such, they don't always have the remit for change or the time to implement it.	The interim director themselves can still 'hold the fort' whilst being a champion of change. Simply bringing up change in meetings and presentations and keeping it on the agenda is 'holding the fort'. Governing bodies should also ideally provide a specific brief.
Interim directors can be in post for too short a time to come to grips with what has been happening, and what needs to happen next (even if they are internally appointed).	Senior managers can support an interim director who does not have the knowledge, skills and experience of change management, although progress may be slow.
Some interim directors don't have the skills and experience, or strategic vision, to understand the change needed – or they are not interested in it.	Governing bodies must identify the interim director's skills and interest to lead change before appointing them.
Some interim directors are brought in to implement a specific change or to get the organisation through a major funding bid. In these cases, the interim director can be quite experienced but not interested in staying longer than it takes to finish that particular task.	An interim director can be effective at kick-starting a change process that is later continued by others.

New directors

Problems	Possible solutions
New director finds that the organisation is not ready for change. Basic functions like finance and staffing need addressing.	The governing body's role is to ensure the new director fully understands where the organisation is and to be realistic about what can be achieved in the short term. But even when examining basic functions, the principles of the organisation and the medium and long-term ambitions for change can be promoted by the new director.
New directors (and interim directors) don't always get the information they need to understand what an organisation is committed to, who is involved and the expectations of funders. They don't understand the history.	Staff should be fully involved in the change process and can support the new director.

(Continued)

Problems	Possible solutions
When a new director arrives, it is not uncommon for some work streams, especially ones that involve change and new ways of working, to pause as staff wait to see which way the director will take the museum.	The new director must make an immediate and public commitment to the change process, and continue to reiterate that commitment at every opportunity. By involving staff in the discussion about change, they will create champions of change and help it to succeed.

See also:

5   Change is everyone's job
15 Governance and change
23 Distributed leadership and sharing decision-making
34 Champions of change

Note

1 R.R. Janes, *Museums and the paradox of change: A case study in urgent adaptation* (third edition, Routledge 2013), p. 186.

23

DISTRIBUTED LEADERSHIP AND SHARING DECISION-MAKING

Experiment with new models of shared, distributed leadership, and be prepared for the work to change who has power in making decisions.
Sarah Lee and Katherine Gean, *The Engagement Revolution*[1]

Leadership, like change itself, is everyone's job, so change should not be solely the preserve of one leader. You must lead yourself, your projects, your own particular staff and volunteers, and contribute to the overall leadership of the museum, supporting your director. Robert Janes refers to this as 'each staff person being a creator of the organization'.[2] The age of the heroic leader has definitely passed, so sharing the leadership responsibilities, especially in a time of major change, is a wise and effective approach. The more staff are involved, the less likely they are to resist, and the more likely change can be successful and sustained.

A board of charity trustees or a political cabinet have collective responsibility. This spirit should carry through any organisation, whatever its structure, so there is effective, shared decision-making. As members of a senior, departmental or project management team, everyone will have their own areas of expertise and arena of responsibility, in effect distributed leadership (providing they are working to the organisation's plan and not creating their own private fiefdom). Devolved or distributed leadership can assist to prevent the change becoming an instrument of dictatorship.

Indeed, an important aspect of the change process at the Oakland Museum of California was to create a new structure that would explicitly move away from the traditional hierarchical top-down model of leadership, to developing leadership throughout the whole organisation. The museum's governing body felt that this would nurture innovation, creativity and risk-taking throughout the organisation – all of which are essential elements in a successful change programme.[3]

In times of crisis, or during a major project which takes all or most of the director's time, everyone else should share the burden of leading, each in their own area of skill. While the final decision on any matter may still rest with the director, this model of leadership shares responsibility. Therefore, it makes for a more effective organisation which can then more readily respond to external forces or imposed changes and, in addition, helps the director or chair to be more effective in their job.

With this model of leadership, there should be several leaders at different levels of the organisation and in different skill areas to implement the change programme. This is more than simply doing lots of delegating. The leadership element means that those individuals have actual authority, within agreed parameters, and are not simply carrying things out on behalf of someone more senior. Robert Janes points out that, in these less hierarchical organisational structures, the role of a traditional manager changes, as they become coaches, mentors and advisers, who encourage rather than control, and motivate rather than order. One thing to look out for is managers refusing to allow staff to assume greater responsibility, for example, by withholding information: delegation and sharing decisions in practice is a skill to be learned, like any other, and some staff may need help with this.[4]

Involving many different types of people in the change programme is an approach which can counter those who are resistant to, or in denial of, the change (see Chapters 31 and 45). However, you should not choose your key team to help you to deliver this change just for this reason, but it could be an added bonus if it converts some sceptics to the changes.

Being democratic about how you lead and manage your museum is also an effective methodology even when you are not engaged in a change programme. Involving your staff in decisions about a new structure, ways of working, programming, finance, whatever the change is about, is an efficient and equitable method of leadership. This is not only distributed management but, if decision-making is also included, it is distributed leadership too. Sharing painful decisions about staffing structures and financial cuts may be seen as a 'cop-out' by some of the staff, but doing so has two main advantages: it increases understanding of the challenges and dichotomies inherent in leading an organisation, and it makes staff feel they are crucial to the life of the museum, so they feel they have equity in it, even without the financial rewards normally associated with that word. Motivation will not be difficult for them if this is the approach, not just to the change programme, but to running the museum in future.

If your leadership is not democratic and coaching in style, this may not be your natural or preferred way of leading the change programme. However, if you take into account the challenges of leading and changing a group of museum professionals – whatever the type and style of your organisation – then you will recognise that this is an effective method of ensuring your leadership is successful in a time of challenge and change. Adapting to this leadership style is possible if you acknowledge its benefits for the success of your change programme.

If this is to be successful, it is essential that clearly established parameters of the shared responsibility for decision-making are understood by all. It does not mean people going away to do whatever they want to do. There will be limits to authority which must be spelled out before being put into practice, and sticking to the agreed change programme will be the over-riding factor.

Beyond the present change programme, this would lead to a more effective and efficient museum overall once the first phase of change is completed.

See also:

11   Be open to challenge and new ideas
24   Involving stakeholders in the change process
34   Champions of change
40   Internal networks and collaboration

Notes

1   S. Lee and K. Gean, *The Engagement Revolution: A study of strategic organizational transformation in 10 California arts nonprofits* (James Irvine Foundation 2017), p. 67.
2   R.R. Janes, *Museums and the paradox of change: A case study in urgent adaptation* (third edition, Routledge 2013), p. 89.
3   G. Anderson, 'Reflections on organizational transformation in the twenty-first century', in R.R. Janes, *Museums and the paradox of change: A case study in urgent adaptation* (third edition, Routledge 2013), p. 197.
4   R.R. Janes, *Museums and the paradox of change: A case study in urgent adaptation* (third edition, Routledge 2013), pp. 48, 91.

24

INVOLVING STAKEHOLDERS IN THE CHANGE PROCESS[1]

Inviting stakeholders to be part of the change process can be a very astute political move and therefore successful in keeping their support, in the same way as involving many different voices (see Chapters 11, 40) and involving the communities you serve or wish to serve (see Chapter 25).

Stakeholders will come in all shapes, sizes and motivations. Museums will have Friends organisations and/or corporate members, and possibly development charities who fundraise for particular capital projects. These are the great and the good of fundraising and range from 'indie givers', who give a thousand pounds (or dollars) at a time in return for particular benefits, to the High Net Worth individuals who have a longer term financial and advocacy relationship with the organisation.

Many stakeholders will have a financial stake in museums, their collections, sites and buildings and may even ultimately own them.[2] Some may be sponsors or funders for particular projects or developments. Some, such as the National Lottery Heritage Fund in the UK, which grant-aids a wide range of projects and museum activity, will ask that the receiving museum sign a contract not only for the duration of the project, but for many years ahead. Others, like the Art Fund or the National Heritage Memorial Fund, would want a contract if they grant-aided the purchase of a particular object, to ensure it would not be disposed of in future without consulting them, and potentially paying back the grant monies.

It is essential that, as with shared decision-making (Chapter 23) and community involvement (Chapter 25), the parameters of the relationship are clearly established at the start and are fully understood by all parties. Particularly where financial support is concerned, there is considerable scope for stakeholders to believe they can influence the direction, style and programming of the museum. So if you are inviting them to be part of the change programme, it must be clear that meddling and interference is not part of the involvement once the programme has been agreed upon by the governing body.

In these cases, including stakeholders in the consultation stages when developing the scope and nature of the change programme can be the most effective approach. If contributing at this stage, your stakeholders are more likely to be advocates for the changes in the future. If there is opposition to some of the changes, then this alternative perspective could be very valuable. Individual stakeholders could bring considerable relevant experience from other sectors to the discussions of change programmes to complement those of the director, the staff and governing bodies (see also Chapter 54).

Notes

1 In this chapter, stakeholders are not a museum's local community – for that, see Chapter 25.
2 For example, in the case of local authorities in the UK where trusts operate their sites, so they are in effect a client, or some sites will have a private landowner from which the museum operates, e.g. Creswell Crags Museum and Heritage Centre in England.

25

COMMUNITY PARTNERSHIPS AND CHANGE

> [T]he museum is incapable of change without the views/voices/input of its community partners as a central element of organisational development.
>
> Bernadette Lynch, *Our Museum*[1]

Many change programmes are a response to a need for the museum to become more relevant to its communities (see Chapter 17). This is often directly linked to long-term financial sustainability, as the organisation attempts to persuade funders and stakeholders that it can make a real impact on people's lives and is worth funding. In these cases, the museum cannot transform on its own: it requires the active collaboration of its communities in a discussion about what they want from their museum, what the mutual benefits might be, what is achievable and their role in the change process.

Effective museum–community partnerships which make a real difference to their communities are more important now than ever before. Many museums will only survive and thrive through working closely with their communities and making a tangible difference. Direct community engagement – *making a difference* – is increasingly a priority for funders, public and private. Museums have resources, space and expertise: they can be a vital part of serving their communities by listening to what they need, and, indeed, what they can offer. This, in turn, can effect further change in the museum.

The power of communities to effect change has been recognised in other sectors. In health and care, for example, there is evidence that communities are the ones with real power to drive innovations, provide new ideas and reshape plans for primary care models and hospital provision.[2] Active partnership with communities is an important element in change for museums too, and they need to allow people to be an effective and integral part of that process.

Effective partnerships with communities

Real partnership with communities is more than just consultation, which can occasionally be tokenistic. At the very least, a partnership means deciding together for mutual benefit. Each museum must identify a diverse range of voices from its own communities, decide how far it is prepared to go in terms of sharing authority and decision-making and of course assess how far its communities would like it to go. Some communities might want to be more actively and strategically involved.

There are common elements in creating sustainable and dynamic partnerships between museums and communities that help drive change.[3]

- Relationships often begin with open conversations about what museums and communities might want to do together. Ideas are then jointly developed, rather than fixed projects imposed by the museum.
- Reflecting on how successful relationships have developed, community partners single out the building of trust, the knowledge that it is not tokenistic but for the long term and constantly developing. But building trust takes time and patience: it is a process that cannot be rushed or fast-tracked. Time needs to be built in to allow for trust to grow at its own pace. The authors' experience is that it takes at least a year for trust to develop in such relationships.
- Museum/gallery programmes are designed around the needs and interests of community partners.
- The partners feel they have agency in decision-making, they feel valued and the relationship with the museum is creative and mutually beneficial.
- The expertise of community partners is recognised and respected. They bring useful knowledge, skills and experience to the museum and might run training workshops for museum staff on aspects where they are more expert.
- Some projects/programmes are led by community partners.
- Community partners feel able to challenge the museum and have the freedom to raise all sorts of issues – although there is acknowledgement that trust is required before partners feel able to challenge.
- A very practical tip! Community partners should always be kept informed, sent minutes of meetings and given feedback about the progress of the project/relationship, the impact of the partnership on the museum and aspirations for the future.

Pitfalls to avoid

Two common pitfalls in relationships between museums and communities are reported by community partners representing a broad range of museums/galleries.

These pitfalls have been termed 'false consensus' and 'rubber-stamping', in which museums deliberately over-emphasise the level of buy-in from communities in order to carry out their own plans and avoid differences of opinion and conflict.[4]

False consensus is where the museum deliberately, or even subconsciously, works with communities that are less challenging, more in keeping with the organisation's priorities and more willing to accede to the museum's goals. The museum convinces the participants that their interests are the same as those of the organisation, leaving no room for robust challenge or dialogue about aims. The effect on partners is to make them feel disempowered and not listened to, and unlikely to repeat the partnership with the museum.

Rubber-stamping is when communities are brought in simply as a means of agreeing and signing off on existing plans already drawn up by the museum, that they have had little or no involvement in shaping. The museum then claims that it has consulted and has community support for its plans.

False consensus and rubber-stamping are not partnership: they are tokenistic consultation, in which the communities have no real voice or agency.

Involving community partners in strategy

The most effective way of involving communities in planning and implementing long-term change is to include them in governance and shared decision-making. That way, they have a real strategic role in change, working with the museum in setting policy, targets, monitoring and evaluation rather than just on short-term projects.

There are different mechanisms through which communities can be involved in wider strategy.[5]

- Community partners sit on the governing body. Their role is not to 'represent' the community or their own organisation, but to bring particular skills and knowledge to contribute to the governance of the museum. Appointing community partners helps diversify a governing body, brings in different skills and perspectives and is one way of keeping track of changing community agendas (see Chapter 17). Of course, not all community partners want to be involved in a museum's governance, and some prefer to continue to work on short-term projects that reflect their own interests.
- Community partners can contribute to strategic discussions through advisory panels or participatory fora that focus on different areas of museum work (see some practical examples of how this might work in Chapter 8). While these may not always be formal layers of decision-making, they bring new expertise and perspectives into the museum, especially if they report regularly to the governing body.
- Community partners can participate in workshops with the museum to develop long-term strategy, in a collaborative process alongside staff, volunteers, trustees and stakeholders (see example in Chapter 8). When this works

well, everyone has the opportunity to contribute and reach consensus about the direction of change.

See also:

24 Involving stakeholders in the change process
52 External voice and critical friends

Notes

1 B. Lynch, *Our Museum: A five-year perspective from a critical friend* (Paul Hamlyn Foundation 2015), p. 3.
2 D. Dougall, M. Lewis and S. Ross, *Transformational change in health and care: Reports from the field* (The King's Fund 2018), pp. 87–88.
3 P. Bienkowski, *Our Museum: What happened next? A review and further learning two years on* (Paul Hamlyn Foundation 2018), pp. 22–23; S. Lee and K. Gean, *The Engagement Revolution: A study of strategic organizational transformation in 10 California arts nonprofits* (James Irvine Foundation 2017), pp. 44–46; N. Sim, 'Findings from the field: Partnership working between galleries and youth organisations', in M. Miller, R. Moilliet and E. Daly (eds.), *Circuit – Test, Risk, Change: Young people, youth organisations and galleries working together* (Tate and Paul Hamlyn Foundation 2019), pp. 40–48. See also ofbyforall.org.
4 B. Lynch, *Whose cake is it anyway? A collaborative investigation into engagement and participation in 12 museums and galleries in the UK* (Paul Hamlyn Foundation 2011), pp. 11–13.
5 P. Bienkowski, *Our Museum: What happened next? A review and further learning two years on* (Paul Hamlyn Foundation 2018), p. 24.

26

CUTS AND DOWNSIZING

Change can often be driven by the need to save money. Salaries and the expenditure associated with employment are by a long way the largest expenditure of any museum, even for smaller museums that only have one or two employees. In order to save money, restructuring has become a norm for achieving required savings (see Chapter 38 for more on this).

Particularly since the global financial crisis of 2008, cuts have been a way of life for the cultural sector. Public funding overall has been in decline ever since and it is now accepted that cultural organisations must raise their own cash to sustain even day-to-day activities.

Local authorities in the UK in particular have been targeted for savings by central governments who since the 1990s have sought to render them more and more harmless. Even within central government, reducing subsidies and close examination of all expenditure have become a way of life. So *doing more with less* has become a mantra for museums as they seek collaboration, external contracts and partnerships to stretch limited resources further.

Short-term contracts have, sadly, become the norm in museums (in every type of museum) as project-funding dictates when staff are hired and fired. This leads to a lack of consistency of understanding about the museum as a whole – why things are the way they are, and even what the museum has committed to with external funders – as the corporate or tribal memory has no shared soil in which to flourish (see Chapter 55). It is also another way of saving money, as employing those staff with particular skills for specific periods of time is more cost effective than having them on the permanent staffing complement.

Downsizing is not only for empty nesters moving to bungalows. Reducing staffing and programme budgets are reliable methods of achieving savings from revenue expenditure. However, this has a knock-on effect of reducing the museum's ability to carry out its collections care and interpretation, activity and outreach programmes, and to staff and run its sites and buildings. Museums in this situation must say *no* to new ideas and opportunities more often as they cannot sustain activity at a high level if the organisation and staffing levels are so much smaller. These museums need to focus on changing their mentality and their ambitions to match their resources, even if they do so reluctantly. If, in addition, the staff are working through a major change programme, then it becomes vital to adjust the activities of the museum to match your ability to pay; otherwise staff will crash and burn out.

See also:

27   Commercialisation and change
38   Restructuring, redundancies and staff changes

27

COMMERCIALISATION AND CHANGE

If *doing more with less* has become a mantra for museums, their funders and governing bodies have often used external contractors as a means to ensure that services continue and to achieve a reduction in their overall revenue and staffing expenditure. The need to generate income and reduce expenditure through an expansion of commercial activities is an increasing element – sometimes the key element – in change programmes. But it can also have an impact on other aspects of change.

Approaches to commercialisation in museums vary in different countries. In most, financial support from government – either direct or through agencies such as Arts Council England and its equivalents – is the largest source of income, often 50 to 70 per cent of total operating revenue. In the USA, Canada and the UK it is usual for museums to generate about 25 to 30 per cent of their income from earned sources.[1]

Independent museums, commercialisation and change

Of course, there are independent museums with no public funding at all, which rely entirely on admission fees, retail, catering, facility rental, events programming, donations, membership programmes and corporate sponsorship. In the USA, there is much lower government support, so most US museums are, effectively, commercial concerns. They often share capital costs with developers and can receive income from ongoing fees. The Museum of Modern Art in New York, for example, paid for its expansion and renovation by allowing a developer to add about 46 floors of condominiums to its six-storey museum, and it continues to receive a portion of the annual fees.

But tensions often arise in boards when proposed changes might disrupt traditional sources of revenue; for example, when a community engagement strategy impacts on marketing to tourists. On the other hand, when traditional revenue sources dry up, community engagement remains as the only viable economic alternative: when that happens, 'selling a product about community is easier to sell than art'.[2] The problems of commercialisation and change then become a question of conflicting priorities (see Chapter 8).

Publicly funded museums, outsourcing and change

The tensions around commercialisation in publicly funded museums tend to revolve around cuts in funding, local authorities divesting themselves of direct responsibility for running cultural venues and the consequent need for museums to generate a larger proportion of their income at the same time as changing their form of governance.

In the UK, many local authorities have contracted out the operation of museums in different ways, often creating independent charitable trusts on the 'arm's length' principle. The new trusts have had fluctuating fortunes and varied experiences. Many of them changed and developed more entrepreneurial and income-generating skills. But the continuing drive for the local authorities to save money, despite funding agreements to enable the trusts to plan financially in the medium term, has caused a strained relationship between local authority parent and museum child. The museum changed but the local authority did not change their view of how they expected the museum to behave, nor understood how the museum could support them in delivering their strategic priorities.

Some aspects of what a museum does are easier to externalise, as they are services that commercial companies provide all the time, such as catering. In 2004, the Victoria & Albert Museum in London was the first UK museum to outsource its catering services to an external company,[3] and now most large museums do the same. In terms of catering, this can make economic sense as museums need specialist skills to prepare and serve food, and the turnover of staff is often high and seasonal. So it can be more cost effective for an external company to provide a museum's catering than for the museum to do so itself. However, not all services a museum provides are so clear cut, easy to specify and with a commercial market equivalent.

Museums are complex creatures with many facets, so the lessons are that while financial benefits for public authorities may be clear cut and easy to understand, museums cannot be treated as a single, simple organism; their different aspects must be taken into account for radical change to be successful and long lasting. Many of the services the museum provides and, in some cases, is required to deliver, are at odds with a more simplistic, commercial approach of public bodies seeking to offload their responsibilities and save money (see Chapters 8 and 48). This is where the pinch point has come for many of the newly 'independent' museum trusts in the UK. Their funders are considering these complex organisations in the same context as simpler, more single-subject organisations such as swimming pools or playing fields.

Whether publicly funded or independent, if part of your stimulus for change is the generation of income and reduction of expenditure through saving on fixed salary costs (see Chapter 7), then outsourcing of some services should be considered. In simple economic terms, it may seem the best solution. But you need to ensure that the external company delivering the service understands the museum's values and ethos and will deliver the services in a fashion that supports those values (see Chapter 19); otherwise, your wider change programme may be undermined. Ultimately, the visiting public does not know or care that catering, or a museum shop, or cleaning are run by a separate company. It will all be part of their experience of the museum as a whole. So make sure that the aims and values of the commercial companies you use are aligned with yours.

See also:

8   Balancing conflicting priorities

Notes

1   T. Silberberg and G. Lord, 'Balancing mission and money: Critical issues in museum economics', in C. McCarthy (ed.), *Museum practice* (Wiley Blackwell 2015), pp. 164–70. In the decade to 2018 in English arts organisations, earned income rose by 47 per cent while local government funding fell by 43 per cent: *Arts Index England 2007–2018* (National Campaign for the Arts 2020).
2   Quoted in S. Lee and K. Gean, *The Engagement Revolution: A study of strategic organizational transformation in 10 California arts nonprofits* (James Irvine Foundation 2017), p. 57.
3   T. Marks, 'The ace caff that now leaves a bad taste – at the V&A Café', *Apollo* (February 2020), p. 16.

28

EMBRACING RISK

Why risk trying something new and innovative — can't things just stay the way they are?

The museum sector is notoriously risk averse. Of course there are understandable reasons for this. Publicly funded institutions need to show that they are being careful and sensible with taxpayers' money, not throwing it away on crazy schemes that are not proven to work and that the media might build up into a scandal (local authorities in the UK are especially sensitive on this matter). Independent museums depend on paying visitors to survive, and sober commercial considerations often outweigh imaginative but potentially risky approaches which do not guarantee income. Sometimes there is simply fear of unknown audiences and populations, especially around opportunities for innovative collaboration: fear of the risk of them having expectations and demands that the museum is not prepared to fulfil.[1]

> [T]he appetite for radical change will be a lot lower if organizational leaders are only interested in changing a program or two.
> Sarah Lee and Katherine Gean, *The Engagement Revolution*[2]

There is often hesitation or resistance to committing to broad organisational change. In the change programme in California cited in the previous quotation, leaders wavered between seeing it as a limited programme which should not pose too much risk to organisational stability, and seeing opportunity for more dramatic change (see also Chapter 37 on overcoming project mentality).

The risk of change is often seen by governing bodies, directors and staff as greater than the risk of standing still. At the Museum of Vancouver, sagging attendance, flat government funding, no support from sponsors or donors and little local awareness of the museum were all long-term symptoms of its increasing lack of relevance to the community, but some staff believed that the status quo could continue without consequence. There was 'a resignation that nothing could change because it was too risky' – because what was required were fundamental changes to programming, staff and structure.[3]

Institutional responses to risk can be subtle, rather than obvious. Sometimes, a response to an innovative and potentially risky approach is not a straight 'no' from leaders or managers, but redirection or a steer towards more acceptable or safer approaches, which are an unconscious symptom of their aversion to risk.[4]

Yet, once a need for change has been identified, the biggest risk is not taking any risk at all. Making a change is all about managing risk. In its change programme, the Royal Shakespeare Company saw it as a duty to experiment and to conduct trials that opened up new, more effective and creative ways of working, because such small-scale innovations helped change to happen[5] (see Chapter 12 on pilot projects). It is true that occasionally such experiments resulted in setbacks, failure and frustration, but they were also a valuable opportunity to learn from mistakes and embed the learning into further experimentation and change.

The *Our Museum* programme in the UK, focused on embedding community participation through organisational change, actively encouraged the confidence to take risks and to be more open to doing things differently – to try things out and to learn from what worked and what didn't. Many of the participating organisations acknowledged that using the word 'pilot' allowed more risk taking, because any risk was perceived by staff, governing bodies and stakeholders to be short-term and could be contained. This approach of piloting alternative solutions was an effective way of trying something new without alarming these constituencies unduly.

Changing things depends on creating confidence and trust. Individual confidence is intangible and difficult to measure, but it is an important factor in change. In the *Our Museum* organisations, confidence grew from trialling different collaborative approaches; feeling able to take a risk; openly discussing what worked well and less well; having a shared understanding of what the organisation was trying to achieve; and, as a result, staff felt empowered to make decisions. Confidence is also a counter to organisational attitudes to risk and blame which lead to a generally risk-averse culture.[6] Similarly, participants in the UK Museums Association's programme *Transformers*, about developing mid-career change agents in museums, reported a growth in their confidence and courage and a feeling of agency within their organisation to make change and to convince others of the importance of that change.[7]

But it is crucial to be clear *why* you are trying something new and potentially risky and to communicate this clearly to everyone – staff, stakeholders, funders and the media. Be proactive and anticipate what their reactions and reservations might be. Do not wait for adverse reactions after the fact, when you will be playing catch-up and reacting to negative media coverage. Take the lead and be in control of your own narrative. Anticipate a worst-case scenario and explain up front what you want to achieve, that you expect some things not to go to plan, and that you have a process in place to learn from any mistakes which will be a valuable contribution to the overall change programme. By providing clarity for your motivations and actions, and showing that you understand the risk and that it is worthwhile, you will assuage most of the alarm from your stakeholders and audiences (see Chapter 39 on communicating change).

See also:

12   Explore and test – the value of pilot projects
29   Don't be afraid to report problems or 'failure'
30   Fear of change
56   Sharing the learning

Notes

1   N. Morse and M. McCann, *Becoming a change-maker in museums: Experiences, opportunities and challenges: Reflections on the Museums Association's Transformers Workforce Development Initiative* (University of Leicester 2019), p. 14.
2   S. Lee and K. Gean, *The Engagement Revolution: A study of strategic organizational transformation in 10 California arts nonprofits* (James Irvine Foundation 2017), p. 38.
3   N. Noble, 'Museum of Vancouver – A transformation in progress', in R.R. Janes, *Museums and the paradox of change: A case study in urgent adaptation* (third edition, Routledge 2013), p. 226.
4   N. Morse and M. McCann, *Becoming a change-maker in museums: Experiences, opportunities and challenges: Reflections on the Museums Association's Transformers Workforce Development Initiative* (University of Leicester 2019), pp. 13–14.
5   R. Hewison, J. Holden and S. Jones, *All together: A creative approach to organisational change* (Demos 2010), pp. 49, 127.
6   P. Bienkowski, *Our Museum: What happened next? A review and further learning two years on* (Paul Hamlyn Foundation 2018), p. 27.
7   N. Morse and M. McCann, *Becoming a change-maker in museums: Experiences, opportunities and challenges: Reflections on the Museums Association's Transformers Workforce Development Initiative* (University of Leicester 2019), p. 7.

29

DON'T BE AFRAID TO REPORT PROBLEMS OR 'FAILURE'

When something goes wrong, I'm the first to admit it, I'm the first to admit it, but the last one to know.

Paul Simon[1]

There is no such thing as failure, only mistakes from which you do not learn.

The heading of this chapter calls this 'failure' in inverted commas for a reason. As your change programme is not one event, but a process, some aspects may not go to plan, without completely undermining the overall programme. Total failure may only occur if the organisation has to abandon the agreed upon process part-way through; even then, you are likely to have achieved some aspects of the change and will have learned a lot about your staff and stakeholders, and probably yourself, whatever your role. This increased knowledge should be documented, analysed and used to plot a fresh course for a new or slightly altered destination.

Admitting you have a problem, however large or small, or even that the change programme has failed, is a mature and adult decision, even if you yourself as director feel that you are to blame for the failure. Most change programmes will encounter problems and some may fail; it is no shame if either of these happen to you, providing you have prepared carefully, assessed risks before you began, and your governing body and executive remain committed to the agreed upon path. Some events are outside your control – global seismic events such as wars, pandemics or major climate catastrophes – but those which can be under your control or influence should be anticipated if possible or reacted to if not (see Chapter 21).

However, not learning from mistakes or apparent failure is not excusable. Funders are increasingly open to organisations admitting when things have not gone to plan, and welcome evidence that you have learned from mistakes. Keeping in mind your initial goal and the reasons why this was the right path will allow you to re-group and agree on an alternative path to your destination.

Problems or 'failure' can be very useful, as they can signal that your approach needs revising (rather than abandoning). The outcome of your change programme may still be valid, but how you get there may need tweaking. For example, one of the aspects that often goes wrong in museum change programmes is getting staff buy-in and support – many museums think that a few emails, newsletters, announcements from the director and a question-and-answer session at a staff meeting are sufficient for staff to understand and support a change programme. Typically, 12 or 18 months into the programme, they realise that this is not the case, and that there is widespread misapprehension and even resistance that threatens to undermine the change. They then have to re-think their whole approach to bringing staff on board (see Chapter 33 for how this can be done successfully: some of the practical examples there were developed after initial 'failure' had prompted a reappraisal).

As change is a (long) process, not a single project, apparent failure should usually be regarded as only a delay, a postponement rather than complete failure. Using your knowledge of why you encountered these problems, you can recast your route to the initial goal you were seeking at the beginning. But this is also an opportunity to ensure that your destination is indeed still the right one, and tweak any details to ensure the change remains potent and relevant.

See also:

17 Staying relevant
21 How to sustain change
37 Overcoming project mentality
56 Sharing the learning

Note

1 'Something so right', from *There Goes Rhymin' Simon*, ©1973.

PART 4

The role of staff and volunteers in change

A key thread running through this book is that change is everyone's job. Anyone can and should be a change agent, not only the director and senior managers. Part 4 focuses on the roles of staff and volunteers during the change programme – how to involve them directly, recognise their concerns and support them. It is very practically focused, as it incorporates top tips and tried-and-tested methods.

It deals with fear of change, and identifying both champions of change and those who are opposed to it. It describes ways of keeping up morale, especially during restructuring and staff changes, and gives practical suggestions on how to communicate what is happening with the change programme, both internally and externally. Emotions will run high at times, especially if staff feel threatened or wish to resist the change, so acknowledging and coping with this is a key part of a leader's job.

30
FEAR OF CHANGE

> Change is scary for the individuals living through it; it brings to the surface both fear of the unknown and fear of being left out.
>
> Sarah Lee and Katherine Gean, *The Engagement Revolution*[1]

Fear is one of the biggest barriers to sustainable organisational change. Hearing 'we've never done it like that before' is the bane of any new museum director's life. Fear can lead to paralysis and avoidance.

Fear of change among staff and volunteers – and also among governing body members and community partners – is normal and to be expected. The authors have encountered fear of risk, fear of being blamed, fear of losing your job, fear of your role being undermined, fear of doing something you don't want to do, fear of the lack of certainty related to financial survival, fear of community participation as a perceived threat to professional expertise and status and fear of an uncertain future that change might bring. There is also fear of looking stupid, both on an institutional and an individual level.

A significant amount of the fear of change is a result of individuals not knowing how they may be affected personally. This is not surprising, as routines of work and life are a way of human beings feeling safe, so disruption can be frightening. An evaluation of change at museums and arts organisations in California found that staff were comfortable with uncertainty related to changes in programming, but less comfortable with changes in roles, titles, relationships and day-to-day responsibilities. A restructure can provoke fear of being left out, which in its turn provokes resistance to the change itself. Those not involved in decisions were anxious about how the changes would affect them personally, while decision makers experienced stress in the knowledge that their choices would have personal consequences for many.[2]

As part of managing this fear, identifying both champions of change (Chapter 34) and those who are opposed to it (Chapter 31) are vital. It is important to accept that fear will exist and neither ignore it nor underestimate its potential impact on staff behaviour. Real fear must be recognised so that you can support those who exhibit it, or it can lead to serious illness.

Change is difficult because it challenges us on many different fronts. The typical reaction to change is in four stages, similar to the stages in bereavement:

- Shock and denial.
- Anger and other emotional outbursts.
- Gradual, resigned acceptance of the 'new normal'.
- Acceptance and slowly moving forward.

Progression through these stages is rarely simple or linear. You may find that staff get stuck in one stage, or advance quickly but then regress. There is often no clear cut, decisive move from one stage to another.

Imposed change is likely to stimulate the greatest fear, with additional resistance over and above other types of change. Involving a varied selection of staff and volunteers in the creation and introduction of the change will be of considerable assistance to limiting or managing resistance and calming fears (see Chapters 11, 23 and 40). Clear and frequent communication about what is happening is vital, although you should expect that, despite open communication, some staff will continue to struggle with the uncertainty and the perceived personal threat of change – even when the need for overall organisational change is accepted.[3]

Dr Paul Gilbert's work with the *Three Circles of Emotional Regulation*[4] provides a guide for managers to help staff members to cope with their fear in these circumstances (see Chapter 32).

See also:

11 Be open to challenge and new ideas
23 Distributed leadership and sharing decision-making
31 Countering resistance to change
35 Keeping up morale during change
40 Internal networks and collaboration

Notes

1 S. Lee and K. Gean, *The Engagement Revolution: A study of strategic organizational transformation in 10 California arts nonprofits* (James Irvine Foundation 2017), p. 35.

2 S. Lee and K. Gean, *The Engagement Revolution: A study of strategic organizational transformation in 10 California arts nonprofits* (James Irvine Foundation 2017), pp. 35–36.

3 G. Anderson, 'Reflections on organizational transformation in the twenty-first century', in R.R. Janes, *Museums and the paradox of change: A case study in urgent adaptation* (third edition, Routledge 2013), p. 200.

4 P. Gilbert, *The compassionate mind: A new approach to life's challenges* (Constable and Robinson 2009).

31

COUNTERING RESISTANCE TO CHANGE

To *do* new is different than to *think* new – some people still can't adapt. Maybe they feel their job is at stake.

Wendy Smith, Glenbow Museum[1]

Staff resistance to change can be conscious or unconscious. It can be poor understanding of the change process itself and what needs to change, lack of interest or problems with staff time and capacity. Sometimes change is perceived as a threat to professional expertise and status, especially when a change process is exploring what skills and abilities are needed in the transformed museum. Staff often resist because they lack the skills to deal with particular kinds of change, for example how to listen to and work with different communities in a participatory way or share decision-making in practice. And, of course, there can be opposition to the very nature of the change itself, along the lines of 'This is not what we should be doing as a museum, and it is not what I came into museums to do'.

However, it needs to be acknowledged that (some) resistance can be useful, as it can indicate potential consequences that have been overlooked, and counter-act complacency. Robert Janes notes that 'scepticism and questioning are integral parts of a well-functioning museum',[2] but it is important to ask whether the resistance is self-serving or of benefit to the wider organisation. There is an important role for staff to provide constructive critique and challenge to leaders and managers, and for managers to be open to such challenge, welcome it as positive rather than negative and not feel threatened by it. The difference between constructive criticism and resistance has to be recognised (see Chapter 11: Be open to challenge and new ideas).

Leaders of change may expect to be supported wholeheartedly by their middle managers, but it has been reported that it is precisely that level of management that is most resistant to change, perhaps because they are more likely to be overwhelmed by bureaucratic tasks and under pressure to achieve set goals. Junior staff and senior managers are often supportive of more radical or innovative ideas, and might make more effective champions or allies (see Chapter 34).[3]

Resistance can manifest itself as passive or active, depending on the individual. It is often rationalised either as altruism – for example opposing the introduction of charges for admission or services on grounds of principle – or adherence to professional standards – for example if the change is a perceived threat to curatorial expertise.[4] If fear amongst staff or volunteers is recognised (see Chapter 30), then it must be understood in order for it not to impede the change process. If there is fear, then there will naturally be resistance, sometimes from unexpected sources. It is important to counter the arguments of those in opposition but to do so with cold, hard facts, and keep emotions out of it as much as possible. Above all, if a leader feels anger themselves, they must *not* show this.

How staff resist

Resisting staff will have two main mechanisms of coping: **escape** or **control**, the same as the *flight or fight* response to danger.

Escape coping is based on avoidance. Staff would take calculated actions to avoid the difficulties of the change, deliberately missing consultation meetings about the change or training related to new ways of working. The extremity of this coping mechanism is taking refuge in alcohol or drugs.

Control coping could be positive and proactive. If staff refuse to behave like a victim of change, they might try to control the process, or at least the impact on themselves. In those cases, you can exploit their opposition and use them as part of the change process. It is essential that you do not ignore the resistance or opposition but harness it to keep your opponents closer to the change process and therefore to you as the change leader (see Chapters 33, 34 and 40). Control coping could also be destructive where the staff try to control the change process and take it over completely, to stop it moving forward.

In practice, most staff are likely to respond to change with a mixture of both mechanisms. Control coping is generally the better option, as it is impossible to avoid the reality of change for long without becoming exhausted or bitter, or both. However, the well-educated and highly motivated museum professional has sometimes been capable of being both for some considerable time and moving into negative control coping. If you are the change leader, this is not an opposition to be taken lightly.

How to counter resistance

Some museums expend considerable time and resources in working with resisters to bring them round. This is not always time and money well spent. Amgueddfa Cymru-National Museum Wales experimented with different ways of tackling staff resistance to participatory working, and found that focusing exclusively on developing staff who were reluctant to change was both time and labour intensive, and even with these investments some staff members were still unwilling or unable to change. It was an inefficient use of time, as staff were getting drawn into a barrier conversation: this is a conversation characterised by defensiveness, self-justification, anxiety, fixed ideas and assumptions, and it tends to be circular in nature and can obstruct progress. They found that a more effective approach was to work solely with staff who had a passion or interest in working in a participatory manner – the champions of change (see Chapter 34). Staff with a positive approach to change return to their own departments enthused with the work being undertaken, and this has a ripple effect on colleagues who may have been previously disengaged.[5]

Involving those resisting the change in making decisions about implementing the programme can also assist in countering attempts at sabotage (see Chapter 23). Resisters are used to expecting opposition, so enlisting their support to ensure that the change is more robust will initially unsettle them. Once they are on the back foot, the change leader(s) can begin to win them round.

Positive thinking is a change leader's most potent weapon. It is invisible to the naked eye of the resister but it has within it a steel core of determination. Resisters are often doom mongers in museums, deploring the impact of whatever the change may be on standards of scholarship, funding, collections care or outreach work. While it is not wise to present major changes as improvements to the museum's service, there will be benefits which may as yet be unknown. If the change is externally imposed, lamenting the situation will not assist the museum to cope with the impact of the change agent.

Positive thinking can, however, support staff and help them not to wallow in despair without it being an overtly jollying along irritation. And it can counteract the considerable amount of negativity spread by the resisters.

See also:

14 What makes a good change leader?
23 Distributed leadership and sharing decision-making
30 Fear of change
34 Champions of change
42 Acknowledging emotions

Notes

1 Quoted in R.R. Janes, *Museums and the paradox of change: A case study in urgent adaptation* (third edition, Routledge 2013), p. 144.
2 R.R. Janes, *Museums and the paradox of change: A case study in urgent adaptation* (third edition, Routledge 2013), p. 365.
3 N. Morse and M. McCann, *Becoming a change-maker in museums: Experiences, opportunities and challenges: Reflections on the Museums Association's Transformers Workforce Development Initiative* (University of Leicester 2019), p. 14.
4 R.R. Janes, *Museums and the paradox of change: A case study in urgent adaptation* (third edition, Routledge 2013), pp. 118–19.
5 P. Bienkowski, *No longer us and them: How to change into a participatory museum and gallery – Learning from the Our Museum programme* (Paul Hamlyn Foundation 2016), p. 26. For barrier conversations and how to overcome them, see A. Gonzalez, *Transformative conversations: The heart of the leadership journey* (Logos Noesis 2015), pp. 35–46.

32

SUPPORTING STAFF AND VOLUNTEERS DURING CHANGE

Supporting staff who have worries and concerns about the impact of the change is important. Organisational change, with its perceived risks of restructuring and possible redundancy, can trigger stress in many staff. Like fear, signs of stress need to be recognised so that managers can react to them.

You should look out for classic symptoms of stress:

- Behavioural changes, where staff do not appear to be themselves, sleep badly or are particularly irritable.
- Physiological reactions, where staff are affected by headaches, stomach pains or nosebleeds from high blood pressure.
- Other more serious health problems, which may need medical intervention to diagnose.

But it is equally important to support staff who do not exhibit classic stress symptoms or show signs of needing help.

Peer group support is to be encouraged, but only if the majority are more positive about the changes and so can provide a positive spin on the situation than one of opposition (see Chapter 40 on how internal networks can provide support). Generally, good mental health support is encouraged by all employers and, if you are a new leader, you should encourage this to flourish. If immediate colleagues can assist initially in supporting stress or being an active listener, then that is an ideal place for support to begin. A friend or close colleague understanding someone's problems can help enormously to share the burden, providing they don't pry or preach, and respect confidentiality. The best support is like coaching: listening, understanding and supporting but not advising.

Most staff are likely not to need external support if the change programme is the main cause of their stress, but if there are other parts of their life which are also adding to their stress, then professional help may be needed. Many smaller museums are unlikely to have easily accessible human resources support, while in other larger museums it may be seen as a management tool and not a support for staff. Peer support can help here, as it can make it easier for someone to get help externally.

Financial stress

Research has shown that money worries are significantly greater than stress about other areas of life. Change programmes often lead to staff anxiety about cuts, downsizing, redundancies and consequent loss of income. It is not unusual during crises for museum staff to be asked to take a pay cut or work fewer days a week. In 2019, surveys showed that 36 per cent of UK employees had financial worries that impacted their mental health, performance and relationships with work colleagues.[1]

Employers can help by incorporating financial educational material into their regular internal communications, for example about financial planning, debt management or state benefits, or make free resources available to employees. By making such material available to their staff, employers provide them with information that may help to alleviate financial worries. Another practical step is to invite a financial expert to give a talk on managing money. Human resources departments can rarely assist with individual financial worries, so you might signpost staff who need support to external organisations that have the expertise to help, for example, in the UK, Citizens Advice, or a number of charities that provide education, information, advice and guidance to help people manage their money well and increase their financial wellbeing.

Stress caused by the change process

The more democratic and distributed style of leadership outlined in Chapter 23 can help to support staff who feel the stress of the change programme. This can assist in creating a feeling of wellbeing and shared experiences within the museum from which all staff will benefit. Change may drive a wedge between leaders and their staff, but it can also have a unifying effect on the staff as a whole.

Counselling and coaching could be available within larger organisations such as local authorities or those with an external company providing human resources advice. During its change programme, when stress levels were high, Glenbow Museum organised formal stress management workshops for staff, delivered by a professional counsellor, as well as opportunities for individual counselling, and offered regular groups such as yoga and walking that help alleviate stress.[2] In more serious cases, occupational health assessments are the route to different types of therapy or psychiatric help.

According to Paul Gilbert's model, people often switch between three different responses to manage their emotions (Figure 32.1),[3] and this provides a guide to managers to help members of staff cope with their fear in these circumstances.

THREE CIRCLES OF EMOTIONAL REGULATION

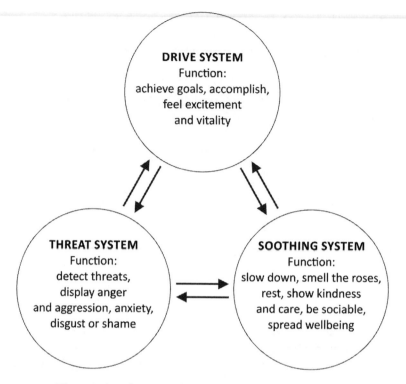

FIGURE 32.1   Three circles of emotional regulation

Most people spend their lives in the Drive and Threat circles. **Drive** is the emotional drive towards purpose, to achieve, to accomplish, to feel excitement and vitality. It makes you want, seek and strive.

The **Threat** circle is the emotional drive to detect threats, so it causes you to display anger and aggression, anxiety, disgust or shame. It makes you want to protect, survive and seek safety. As a result of spending time in both these circles, once the pressures of fear are present, distress is magnified.

The **Soothing** circle is the emotional drive to slow down, smell the roses, rest, show kindness and care, be sociable, give and receive affection and spread wellbeing.

An exercise any manager could carry out is to ask someone to draw their three circles and consider the relative sizes of all of them; then address how they can work towards making them the same size. Evening out the time spent in all three emotional circles helps to ensure the person has a more balanced emotional state. While the director may feel they need a professional to use this, a human resources professional could use it and help the staff member to interpret the findings.

See also:

Notes

1   *The Employer's Guide to Financial Wellbeing 2019–20* (Salary Finance 2019), p. 4. This is a very useful resource, updated annually, with lots of practical tips.
2   R.R. Janes, *Museums and the paradox of change: A case study in urgent adaptation* (third edition, Routledge 2013), p. 71.
3   Adapted from P. Gilbert, *The compassionate mind: A new approach to life's challenges* (Constable and Robinson 2009).

33

STAFF/VOLUNTEER DEVELOPMENT AND CHANGE

> Training is also critical to successful organizational change, as our staff are being asked to develop new ways of working.
>
> Robert Janes, *Museums and the Paradox of Change*[1]

Depending on the nature of your change programme, you will need to consider what you are asking your staff and volunteers to do – both during the change process and afterwards – that is different and new. Do not expect them to work in new ways without development and training. Some will be scared of the proposed changes and will be concerned that their existing knowledge, skills and experience are either insufficient or no longer valued and necessary (see Chapter 30: Fear of change). This may lead them to resist the changes. For the changes to be embedded and sustained, all staff need to understand how they affect their own work and the museum overall, and how they can contribute personally.

Here are examples of new skills and ways of working that are not necessarily covered by standard professional training and that staff might need to develop.

- Working in cross–disciplinary teams.
- Distributed leadership and decision-making.
- Taking on wider roles and responsibilities, for example, specialist curators being more involved in outreach and education.
- Participatory working with communities.
- Facilitation.
- Interpersonal communication.
- Social media communications (nowadays a skill needed by all staff, not just marketing departments).

Research has shown that, in the early stages of a change programme, museums often find it difficult to communicate the aims of the programme and their own strategic objectives.[2] There is a common perception that the change programme is 'just an additional project', one of the many discrete externally funded projects that staff are accustomed to undertaking (see Chapter 37: Overcoming project mentality). The significance of organisational change, and the intention of making overall changes to the museum's policies and practice through the change programme, are often not fully understood. Some staff mistrust the term 'organisational change', believing it to be management speak for a programme of redundancies.

There is a variety of ways of addressing these challenges. Some museums draw in a wider range of staff by inviting them to be part of 'diagonal slice' teams managing the change programme (see Chapters 10 and 11). A traditional approach has been to send staff on off-the-shelf courses, often accredited, to develop new skills, such as project management, facilitation or customer service. Making such courses mandatory can backfire, and it is sometimes a better approach for staff to identify their own training needs, perhaps from a menu of opportunities provided by the museum.

Other museums have developed innovative programmes of continuing professional development to introduce staff to new ways of thinking and working. For example, Glasgow Museums introduced its programme *Staff Ambassadors* to develop all-staff buy-in, understanding and skills around community engagement and participation, which was at the core of their change programme. They needed staff to understand that this was fundamentally about changing the way they worked with communities – and that this was not just a project, but a new way of working that was to become the norm. Very different in approach to traditional training, *Staff Ambassadors* was a self-directed programme, with staff choosing from a menu of opportunities: field visits to community arts projects, involvement in live projects, work swaps, coaching and mentoring. It changed the way staff across a large and complex organisation understood the purpose of their work and that of their colleagues, and increased their confidence, skills and knowledge of working in a more collaborative way. Significantly, it created staff champions for participatory work right across the museum (see Chapter 34).[3]

Other museums have used reflective events such as residentials and facilitated workshops to involve a wider range of staff, to discuss and explore what they were trying to achieve – and, during the change programme, to learn what was working, what wasn't and what they might have to do differently (see Chapter 51: Reflective practice).

A sector-wide approach to developing change agents has been *Transformers*, run by the UK Museums Association.[4] This aimed to equip participants with the tools and resources to be agents of change in their museums. It included year-long training, with residentials and funding to enable professional development and pilot projects. Significantly, participants came from a wide variety of museum roles: education, front-of-house, security, curatorial, collections management, public relations and communications departments, as well as volunteers and interns. This demonstrates that the whole range of professional roles and specialisms is necessary to make change successful and sustained.

Change is everyone's job, and development and training should ensure that everyone in the museum has the right understanding and skills to implement change and to be an active change agent.

See also:

8 Balancing conflicting priorities
11 Be open to challenge and new ideas
19 Values, behaviours and cultural change
20 Building trust

Notes

1 R.R. Janes, *Museums and the paradox of change: A case study in urgent adaptation* (third edition, Routledge 2013), p. 96.
2 G. Moriarty and S. Medlyn, *Our Museum special initiative: An evaluation* (Paul Hamlyn Foundation 2016), pp. 96–97.
3 P. Bienkowski, *No longer us and them: How to change into a participatory museum and gallery – Learning from the Our Museum programme* (Paul Hamlyn Foundation 2016), p. 25, ourmuseum.org.uk/staff-ambassadors/.
4 N. Morse and M. McCann, *Becoming a change-maker in museums: Experiences, opportunities and challenges: Reflections on the Museums Association's Transformers Workforce Development Initiative* (University of Leicester 2019). This evaluates the programme between 2014 and 2018.

34

CHAMPIONS OF CHANGE

Change agents (staff who embraced the change) . . . became critical to boosting morale from within.

Gail Anderson[1]

The most prominent and vocal champion of change must be the director – without that active championing from the top, change will certainly fail (see Chapter 14 on leading change). The governing body, too, needs to be champions in order for change to be embedded and sustained (see Chapter 15: Governance and change).

But leaders need allies within the organisation. Without a broad range of staff supporting and championing the change, it has little chance of success in the long term. Champions are the staff and volunteers who understand the need for change, buy into it, and enthusiastically support it. It is vital to harness the power of these champions and involve them in shaping and managing the change programme, because they are the ones who will effectively disseminate it to other staff and bring those other staff on board.

Chapter 31 on countering resistance to change noted the advantage of working with staff with a positive approach, as it has a ripple effect on colleagues who may be sceptical of the change programme. This organic process of bringing staff and volunteers on board has been described using the analogy of a river. The new way of working is like the water, carrying the positive work and impacts with it. Staff who are unwilling to change are like rocks in the river: the water can't displace them so instead flows around them. Over time, the water wears down the rock, or, as the current of the new way of working gets stronger, it can eventually move the rock. When this happens, former resisters can become champions themselves.[2]

Ideally, your champions will reflect a cross-section of the museum, and so all departments will contain enthusiastic advocates. Allies can have many different origins, so the staff or volunteers who are enthusiastic for change may astonish you. Often, champions will volunteer to be involved in shaping the change. So be open minded about who could be your allies, and welcome any offer of championing, even if you are sceptical as to how effective they may be – prepare to be surprised.

Often new staff members are more supportive as they can clearly see that change is needed. As recent arrivals, they may benefit more from the changes or may have been appointed to support the change process. However, guard against any new-ish staff member who is eager to support the changes becoming a teacher's pet, or appearing to become so. This can disadvantage them, upset longer standing members of staff and make it more difficult to treat them the same as their colleagues.

The change leader should use their champions with care, however. Ensure that no one ever says to one of them 'X is getting you to do their dirty work, then?' In this scenario, the leader is not visible enough or the champion is over-enthusiastic, or both. As with involving stakeholders in change (see Chapter 24), parameters need to be agreed upon so no one can appear to be doing the change leader's job. Even if the leader has not asked them to do so, the staff will immediately think that they have delegated some sensitive task to someone else, when the leader themselves should have shouldered the responsibility.

Whoever they are, these champions need appreciating and nurturing. This means being open to constructive criticism from them. Being a champion of change does not mean agreeing with every aspect of the change programme and how it is being implemented. Enthusiastic champions of change from among the staff and volunteers will often have their ears to the ground and will be in a position to suggest different and better ways of doing things (see Chapter 11: Be open to challenge and new ideas). Being prepared to listen to their suggestions will boost their morale and confidence, and reinvigorate their support for change.

See also:

11 Be open to challenge and new ideas
48 Museum processes as a barrier to change

Notes

1 G. Anderson, 'Reflections on organizational transformation in the twenty-first century', in R.R. Janes, *Museums and the paradox of change: A case study in urgent adaptation* (third edition, Routledge 2013), p. 201.
2 P. Bienkowski, *No longer us and them: How to change into a participatory museum and gallery – Learning from the Our Museum programme* (Paul Hamlyn Foundation 2016), p. 26.

35

KEEPING UP MORALE DURING CHANGE

> It has been a long, exhausting, searching kind of experience that has made us all question our values, our professionalism, our futures.
>
> Donna Livingstone, Glenbow Museum[1]

Maintaining morale throughout the process is important. That is clearly an obvious truth, but if you are a leader concentrating on the change, it is easy to forget. Not everyone has your belief in the change, and many staff may be discouraged or get depressed. Demotivation is contagious, so it could affect many staff quickly.

There is a management cliché that 'morale is very low', and we all hear it too frequently to always take it seriously. However, during a time of upheaval, if staff are unsettled, do not feel valued and stress levels are high, morale may indeed be low at times (see Chapter 32).

An organisation undergoing fundamental or widespread change is likely to be an organisation under pressure; certainly its staff are going to feel the strain. Continuing to do the day job is important as the public service of a museum must not buckle under the internal pressures of a change programme. It is an essential part of leadership to ensure this does not happen. Addressing these pressures is key, as the values of the organisation will be under the microscope during the change programme and behaviours of many staff may be unexpected or unusually disruptive.

It is important that as a leader you remain calm and positive about the changes and the upheavals. Concentrate on being a swan, gliding serenely along even if paddling strongly beneath the water. If you appear to be floundering, then staff will start to question both if you know what you are doing and if this change programme is the right thing to be implementing. While being swan-like may not calm some staff, you will appear to have confidence in your own leadership ability to succeed. This in turn may boost your own belief in your abilities and your own morale. The following passage, from the account of organisational change at Glenbow Museum, highlights the importance of leaders' own morale and how it affects staff morale:

> Paradoxically, and contrary to conventional wisdom, the problem is not only raising the morale of the staff, but ensuring that executives and managers raise their *own* morale. In so doing, they are more likely to develop a creative and productive organization, as managerial effectiveness will grow as their respect for their staff grows. This requires that executives and managers must act in ways which allow their respect for staff to grow.[2]

Demonstrating respect for staff during the upheaval of change is vital. Your front-of-house (FoH) staff, museum assistants or explainers – whatever you call them – have had more prominence in recent years in the sector's press. They are probably the most important staff or volunteers of all: these are the people whom *all* visitors actually meet. You may be a fabulous director, but if your meet-and-greet, retail and catering staff are grumpy and scruffy, then they will give you a reputation for bad service and a poor welcome. This will spread on Tripadvisor and some visitors will arrive expecting it – or will choose not to come at all. If morale is low, then it will be obvious to all of the public, and the strains of the change programme will only exacerbate this situation. While more senior staff may have the ears of influential stakeholders, it is the FoH staff, who meet such a wide variety of people, who will spread the wrong messages about the change. So spend time talking and listening to them.

During a time of stress about change, MBWA – Management by Walking About – has never been more important and you cannot be seen too often (see Chapter 21). Staff will get used to this, but initially it might make them nervous unless your predecessor did it too. Getting used to seeing you out and about makes it easier for them to approach you about an idea or a delicate problem. They may feel that, in the stresses of a change programme, their views and feelings are not being represented, so talking directly to you is a way of ensuring you are alerted to their worries. This should be a real concern for you, especially if unions are involved as, if members are not happy with their representation, you need to know this. So if one or two of them come to you to talk quietly, you must listen.

Knowing you are approachable about major worries will be a considerable boost to morale in general for all staff and volunteers, both now and in the future.

See also:

20 Building trust
30 Fear of change
41 The importance of conviviality
42 Acknowledging emotions

Notes

1 Quoted in R.R. Janes, *Museums and the paradox of change: A case study in urgent adaptation* (third edition, Routledge 2013), p. 149.
2 R.R. Janes, *Museums and the paradox of change: A case study in urgent adaptation* (third edition, Routledge 2013), p. 165.

36

SILO-WORKING

Silo-working is defined as departments, teams or groups in an organisation purposely not working together or sharing information and knowledge with other parts of the same organisation. It is an attitude found in many sectors and organisations of all sizes. That silos are still a barrier to change in museums and other cultural organisations today is well documented.[1]

In museums, there are two causes of silo-working. One is a side-effect of bureaucratic structures and departmental divisions. The second, perhaps unique to museums, is self-created, when some specialist museum staff focus on their own subject areas to the exclusion of the wider work of the museum. Whatever the cause, silo-working is a danger to your change programme, especially if staff resisting the change retreat further into their silos.

In silos created through organisational structures, departmental divisions keep colleagues and departments apart in different ways: physically (occasionally locating some departments in completely different buildings), through the targets they are required to meet, or the specialist teams they work with and through the hierarchy of management reporting systems. Ironically, some progressive organisations have flattened hierarchies to give people more responsibility and to improve performance, but in the process have created silos that have little contact with each other and different ways of doing things.

Self-created silos are not unusual in museums. Many museum professionals are natural silo-workers by inclination and background. They often have an academic background: they are knowledgeable about their subject areas and highly motivated to know and research more, and deliver this knowledge to the public in exhibitions and publications. The public are seen through the lens of their knowledge or when object enquiries demand their attention. Many find it difficult to communicate at a more general level but can enthuse even young children with the detailed wonders of the collections.

But silos are not limited to curatorial departments. There are examples of silos in education and outreach departments, often those with a reputation for innovative ways of working, but who jealously guard their special status and assume that things can only ever be done their way, and any other way is wrong.

These factors create a silo mentality that is a barrier to change, as staff may wish to just focus on, guard and preserve their own specialist area or way of working and be unwilling or uncomfortable working across boundaries to engage with change. In this way, knowledge, resources and even access to collections are not easily accessible across the organisation. In the worst-case scenarios – seen by the authors in many museums – silos can become a museum within a museum: with locked doors preventing access for other colleagues, separate work programmes, non-engagement with the work of the rest of the museum, and non-attendance at staff meetings.

There are two tried and tested ways to counter silos. The first is through creating and supporting internal networks which cut across departmental boundaries. These bring together the allies and champions of change, but also help the silo-workers understand the important work that others in the organisation do, and that they have their own specialist knowledge, skills and experience – *expertise* – which is just as valid as that of the silo-worker (see Chapter 40 on internal networks).

The second strategy is to involve a diagonal slice of staff in the discussion about change (see Chapter 11). This will introduce silo-workers to the wider priorities of the museum, and encourage them to be involved in shaping change. It is a recognition that their expertise and experience is not limited to their own specialist area. Even if individual silo-workers do not take part, there will be a ripple effect across the museum from colleagues with a wider perspective and a positive approach to change which, over time, will help break down the silos (see Chapter 31).

See also:

38   Restructuring, redundancies and staff changes
48   Museum processes as a barrier to change

Note

1   See R. Hewison, J. Holden and S. Jones, *All together: A creative approach to organisational change* (Demos 2010), pp. 123–24; N. Morse and M. McCann, *Becoming a change-maker in museums: Experiences, opportunities and challenges: Reflections on the Museums Association's Transformers Workforce Development Initiative* (University of Leicester 2019), pp. 11–13.

37

OVERCOMING PROJECT MENTALITY

Many staff view a change programme as just another project among myriad other projects, with a defined beginning, middle and end to be delivered to a timescale and budget, not one which will involve and affect the whole organisation and potentially may need to last a long time. Sustaining momentum and the enthusiastic support of the champions over the long haul is hard to achieve, but is an important element of successful change.

Short-term contracts have, sadly, become the norm in museums (in every type of museum) as project-funding dictates when staff are hired and fired. As a result, many staff automatically think of their working lives in terms of time-limited projects, even if they are not on a short-term contract. The funding of such projects dictates the pace of life and the speeding up and winding down of your workload. While a change programme may have phases, the work should not ebb and flow like this but be a continuum.

This mentality leads to a lack of understanding about the museum as a whole, as the corporate or tribal memory has no shared soil in which to flourish. Different project-based staff come and go and don't usually take time to understand why the museum runs as it does; their horizons are prescribed by the limits of their project.

Short-term contracts are also another way of saving money, as only employing staff with particular skills for specific periods of time is more cost effective than having them on the payroll all the time.

All these elements will only reinforce the feelings amongst the staff that the change programme is a project, admittedly a Big Project, but a project nonetheless.

> Improved methods of working in partnership are hard to shift. It sometimes feels easier to revert to the habit of planning and delivering a project straight away.
> Mark Miller, Rachel Moilliet and Nicole Jones, *Circuit*[1]

So why is it dangerous to be in a project mentality instead of a change one?

To be effective, change must have a lasting impact on the organisation as a whole. It must go on making the museum a stronger, more sustainable and more effective organisation. And it must permeate every part of a museum's work, not just affect one aspect or one group of staff. So a good way of countering project mentality is to ensure that everyone understands that it is part of their job – not just that of a small project team. Involving all staff, volunteers, community partners and stakeholders in the change process helps break out of the project box. In many ways, a change programme should be regarded as partnership, not project working.

Not only is the impact of a change process different but its timescale will be too, as the programme may have distinct phases, be tailored to fit peaks and troughs of the museum's work programme, and delays in delivery may occur as new staff are appointed or moved within the organisation. Most importantly, it needs to affect everything, and so it should be expected that it will take up a lot of your time, be you the director or a part-time staff member.

The danger of seeing it as a quick fix is that some may be impatient about the speed of the changes, and some who are opposed may seek to slow it down even further as part of their sabotage. It must not be seen as a distraction from the day job. Momentum may be more difficult to build up and to maintain in these cases too. A change leader must constantly be on their toes to spot these signs in order to shake staff out of their default setting of a project mentality, while staff and volunteers should approach a change programme as an overarching framework that encompasses and affects all their individual projects.

See also:

Note

1   M. Miller, R. Moilliett and N. Jones, *Circuit – Test, Risk, Change* (Tate and Paul Hamlyn Foundation 2017), p. 36.

38

RESTRUCTURING, REDUNDANCIES AND STAFF CHANGES

> Some staff simply won't be up for the kind of radical cultural change, and its implications for their responsibilities, that organizational transformation represents.
>
> Sarah Lee and Katherine Gean, *The Engagement Revolution*[1]

The day-to-day life of the museum or gallery must continue during the change process, and everyone must accommodate the demands the day job makes of them. The challenges of this may mean that externally imposed financial constraints lead to restructuring, staff redundancies and role adjustments that will need to be incorporated into the change timetable. Some staff or volunteers may leave of their own accord, and some because the change programme does not suit their values and way of working. New projects and grants towards specific pieces of work may mean that different work priorities for some staff dictate that roles are changed or adjusted as a result, independent of the change programme. It can be difficult to remain committed to a change journey amidst the constant disruption of key members of staff leaving or changing.

While many change programmes are stimulated by the need to save money or generate additional revenue, often the underlying issue is about refocusing the purpose and approach of the museum so that it addresses community and funders' needs and is able to attract sustainable support and more varied funding[2] (see Chapter 8 for more on this). If this is the case, then solutions are often in the hands of the museum professionals themselves, not their funders. Change programmes are often about what staff do and how they do it, so some form of restructuring is almost inevitable.

A management structure common to many museums is the hierarchical model of top-down leadership supported by isolated departments, each focusing on one primary area of activity, which encourages autocratic decision processes. The Oakland Museum of California found that this traditional hierarchical structure was at odds with the museum's goals and values and hindered its ability to be more agile and responsive. The purpose of restructuring was to align with its goals and values: to put visitor experience and community at the centre of all museum operations and to be porous to the public and community – and the new structure was not static but meant to be tweaked and adjusted.[3]

At the Museum of Vancouver, after years of falling visitor numbers, a public consultation clarified what the museum's communities wanted. As a result, a set of core values and a new vision underpinned the transformation of the museum, leading to an examination of what skills and abilities they needed to achieve the new vision. A complete restructure eliminated all three existing curatorial positions and created new posts with different responsibilities.[4]

The impact of restructures

Restructuring is often a way of life as budgets and demands on museums put pressure on all revenue expenditure. Those who rely on public funding face regular challenges to do more with less, but also to deliver it with fewer people. Restructuring and the threat of redundancies are deeply unsettling for all staff. In addition to other types of change, many will feel destabilised and exhibit signs of stress and anxiety as a result.

Redundancies are sad, especially if the individuals are popular figures, but this does not mean they have a role in the museum's new future; indeed, they may not be very proficient at their current job. Popularity and effectiveness do not necessarily go hand-in-hand. All staff may not recognise this, but a leader must not let emotion about personalities sway their judgement.

Restructures, redundancies and staff changes can lead to a number of problems:

- reduced staff capacity
- lack of continuity with current commitments and external partners
- lack of continuity with funding bodies
- gaps in organisational learning and memory.

The challenge is to ensure that the museum as a whole understands the change programme and that all staff are involved. It is essential that there are good internal communications on current commitments, and that institutional (rather than personal) relationships are maintained with community partners and stakeholders. The change and learning need to be embedded in the institutional memory and not simply reside in key individuals who may have left or been moved to other roles (see Chapter 55).

New staffing structures, new working patterns and relationships and new people may be a result of the change being implemented. All of these may be unsettling to existing staff and so increase apprehension for the organisation as a whole. New appointments coming into the museum during this process may need extra support from the director if their colleagues are negative, in denial or opposing some or all of the change.

Everyone in a position of leadership should recognise that staffing changes unsettle employees, so the change programme will exert additional pressure upon them. Defensive mechanisms then become the overwhelming response, often fuelled by indignation if one of their friends is threatened. In this situation someone could turn from being either ambivalent or merely sceptical about the change programme to being an outright resister.

There are rules about consultation regarding staffing changes of any type, so the change leader must always abide by these.[5] The danger here is that the director could spend a significant amount of their time in these formal meetings and may, as a result, take their eye off the ball and/or lose sight of the overall change destination. It is vital that the director does not lose focus or determination. If you are a member of the governing body supporting them, remember the variety of differing pressures upon your director; they are not treading a straight line but must negotiate round many obstacles, both legal and ethical.

See also:

22 Change of director during the change process
26 Cuts and downsizing
31 Countering resistance to change
35 Keeping up morale during change

Notes

1 S. Lee and K. Gean, *The Engagement Revolution: A study of strategic organizational transformation in 10 California arts nonprofits* (James Irvine Foundation 2017), p. 24.
2 P. Bienkowski, *No longer us and them: How to change into a participatory museum and gallery – Learning from the Our Museum programme* (Paul Hamlyn Foundation 2016), p. 5; N. Simon, *The art of relevance* (Museum 2.0 2016).
3 G. Anderson, 'Reflections on organizational transformation in the twenty-first century', in R.R. Janes, *Museums and the paradox of change: A case study in urgent adaptation* (third edition, Routledge 2013), pp. 192–204.
4 N. Noble, 'Museum of Vancouver – A transformation in progress', in R.R. Janes, *Museums and the paradox of change: A case study in urgent adaptation* (third edition, Routledge 2013), pp. 226–34.
5 For a detailed case study of managing layoffs in a museum, see R.R. Janes, *Museums and the paradox of change: A case study in urgent adaptation* (third edition, Routledge 2013), pp. 65–69.

39

COMMUNICATING CHANGE, INTERNALLY AND EXTERNALLY

> You simply cannot communicate too much.
> Robert Janes, *Museums and the Paradox of Change*[1]

As the leader of change, consider how best to communicate in the coming weeks. Internal communication will be vital to keep all staff and volunteers up to date. Rumour and murmuring gossip will fill any gaps and could destabilise the change overall, so you need to avoid these at all costs.

Plan ahead, do not wing it. For effective communication in these circumstances, you need to make sure that your messages are clear, concise and accurate. This will avoid misunderstandings and ensure that your messages get through at every stage of the change programme. Do not assume that a single all-staff email is sufficient – you need to use every conceivable method of communication to ensure the message about change gets through and is understood. Constantly reiterate the change message at every opportunity, so everyone understands that it is a priority.

Staff/volunteers who do not work full time Monday to Friday may not be able to attend briefings or staff discussions and so can quickly feel 'out of it' and ignored. Consider introducing new staff meetings, discussion groups, emails, newsletters pinned onto staff notice boards and/or a WhatsApp group (or similar).

If you have elderly volunteers who don't 'do' technology, do not suggest they should learn just to suit yourself. Ask one of your trusted lieutenants to print out copies of messages or newsletters for them and put them through their letterbox on the day they are issued. Ensure you write a note so they understand that this has come from you as the leader, what the contents are, what the status is and who else has a copy. If the volunteer is on duty in the museum that day, give it to them directly, in an envelope. Ensure no one feels left out.

Above all, ensure that your communications strategy is inclusive and flexible.

- Do not be economical with the truth but truthful – do not withhold information unnecessarily.
- Use clear and concise language that can be understood by all.
- Do not use jargon or acronyms.
- Ensure it is always correct and complete, so the reader will not be left hanging with several questions once they have read it.

External communication will also be important for stakeholders, Friends groups, community partners and the general public. Think carefully if there is to be a difference between the information given to staff and that provided externally. In situations where staff might feel anxious about change, it is difficult to keep matters confidential. Some staff may confide in a member of the Friends, for example, who may confront you. Beware of betraying confidential assessments or future plans in these circumstances. Never tell a stakeholder anything that is not readily available elsewhere.

You will also need to brief your governing body, as trustees especially will have contact with staff in the normal course of their duties. If they are lobbied about details, do not let them become caught in a 'he said, she said' discussion. Governing bodies should always have a statement on any sensitive topic that they can use if in a tight spot with staff, the press or a zealous member of the Friends.

If embarking on a major change programme, prepare a public communication plan and brief the media beforehand. Anticipate what the media and public reaction might be and be proactive in addressing any concerns: be aware that your aim is to minimise any damage to the museum's reputation and public trust. As always, rumour and conjecture will fill any gaps, so you must show that you are in control of the situation, and have answers prepared concerning why you are undergoing change, the timescale, resource implications and any potential job losses.[2]

As a staff member or a volunteer, be proactive in finding out about any planned changes. Read what is available, ask for information, ask questions and find answers. If you are uninterested or too passive, then you will have no control over what changes happen to you. Make sure you are well informed, talk to managers and colleagues, and take responsibility for your part in the change process.

See also:

35 Keeping up morale during change

Notes

1 R.R. Janes, *Museums and the paradox of change: A case study in urgent adaptation* (third edition, Routledge 2013), p. 123.
2 For a case study on a public communication plan concerning radical change in a museum, see R.R. Janes, *Museums and the paradox of change: A case study in urgent adaptation* (third edition, Routledge 2013), pp. 72–74.

40

INTERNAL NETWORKS AND COLLABORATION

What we talk about is what we become. How we talk – and listen – shapes the possibilities for organizational innovation.

Darren Peacock[1]

An internal network is usually defined as connecting with colleagues within your organisation even if your job does not require you to do so. Such networks are informal and organic. In any organisation there will be groups of staff who are natural allies and friends. You might work with them, or meet up informally during working hours or socially. These informal networks influence the way organisations work and are a significant factor through which change can be achieved.

The most extensive research on internal networks in a cultural organisation has been at the Royal Shakespeare Company.[2] During its change programme, new and strengthened networks helped it to operate to better effect. Over three years, mapping of internal networking revealed improved collaboration and internal resilience. The networks became denser, with more connections, more frequent contacts, and a more evenly balanced pattern of connections across the organisation and across hierarchies – for example, greater connections and more frequent working between the artistic and administrative sides of the organisation. The conclusion was that these informal networks had a measurable impact on the way the organisation worked and how it adapted to change. They helped build a common culture and shared values. Significantly, senior managers were central to these networks – including social ones – and therefore were seen by members of staff as accessible and approachable.

It is therefore important to create an environment within which internal networks can grow and flourish. There are many benefits to the change process of internal networks:[3]

- Networks encourage the development and sharing of ideas and innovation – they help create links that allow things to happen within the organisation.
- Networks allow participants to gain insight into other parts of the museum – what others do, recognising their expertise, the intricacies of different jobs and how they affect each other, and how you can help one another.
- Networks cut across organisational boundaries and hierarchies.
- Networks stimulate collaboration and help overcome silos (see Chapter 36).
- There is evidence that network participants feel more energised in collaborations with colleagues.
- Networks provide support for individuals and allow them to flourish within a group.
- Evidence points to a lower rate of staff turnover where there are flourishing networks, because team members feel connected and have a clearer picture of the organisation's values and purpose.

As a director or a member of staff who sees the need for change, as a first step, learn to identify who your (potential) allies are in the museum. Who are the (potential) resisters, and what strategies could you use to influence them? Directors and other change agents should consider using existing alliances, friendships and work groups as tools in the change programme, and also to broaden the discussion about change. Those who already know each other well should be more effective at working together as part of the implementation team(s). Using existing networks and alliances is an effective way to reassure people unsettled by the change process, as they will be working alongside people they know well, and possibly trust. If change is to be successful, then ensuring that many different viewpoints are taken into account can help, both in its creation and in its implementation. Involving different types and levels of staff and volunteers counters resistance and encourages understanding of the wider perspective of the change programme (see Chapter 11).

However, networks are not always positive and benign. Existing channels of communication and alliances can also be used to subvert a change programme, as staff use their contacts both internally and externally to lobby and try to influence. So directors should be aware of the existing relationships between staff or between staff and a Friends group, for example, as these channels may be a route for sabotage or fake news about the change programme.

See also:

20 Building trust
23 Distributed leadership and sharing decision–making
24 Involving stakeholders in the change process
31 Countering resistance to change

Notes

1 D. Peacock, 'Complexity, conversation and change: Learning how museum organizations change', in R.R. Janes, *Museums and the paradox of change: A case study in urgent adaptation* (third edition, Routledge 2013), p. 242.

2 R. Hewison, J. Holden and S. Jones, *All together: A creative approach to organisational change* (Demos 2010), pp. 81–93, 121–24.

3 See also N. Morse and M. McCann, *Becoming a change-maker in museums: Experiences, opportunities and challenges: Reflections on the Museums Association's Transformers Workforce Development Initiative* (University of Leicester 2019), pp. 11–12.

41

THE IMPORTANCE OF CONVIVIALITY

We work hard, we deserve to laugh.

Lemn Sissay[1]

Conviviality is about creating and facilitating opportunities and circumstances in which the museum can come together informally. This encourages conversations and communication between people from different departments, and an informal sense of togetherness that allows for light-hearted forms of interaction, humour and workplace friendships.

The importance of conviviality is not to be underestimated. Ensuring that spirits are kept as high as possible during the change process will be a challenge, vital to not only maintain morale but to ensure that staff feel like human beings, not numbers on a spreadsheet or a rota.

As part of its change process, the Royal Shakespeare Company created more opportunities for its staff to meet informally. This was done in a number of ways. The design of the premises was changed to ensure that people could meet by chance. Staff catering facilities were redesigned so that as many staff as possible could eat together (instead of eating sandwiches at their own desks). Lots of clubs sprang up: gardening, yoga and a choir. These helped break down hierarchical barriers and created links between different areas. Staff appreciated these opportunities to meet others and find out about them and their roles.[2]

Such opportunities to make people feel welcome and included – as *people*, and not just as staff with particular roles and job descriptions – become even more important as workplaces become increasingly diverse as a result of migration and other socioeconomic changes. For many, the workplace can be the most significant place of interaction with people from different backgrounds. Opportunities for conviviality help with the complexities of interaction with other groups at work.[3] However, such opportunities need to be inclusive: some initiatives can be counter-productive and even divisive if certain staff are unable to attend because of work commitments.[4]

It is important not to go over the top in arranging informal get-togethers, jollying everyone along as though you're celebrating. So keep it appropriately low key, marking significant birthdays of staff, anniversaries of the museum or of a local benefactor. Success from an exhibition with record visitor numbers or a high level of press interest could also be marked to thank the staff who created it and those who staffed the displays and events programme, especially if they had to cope with unusually high numbers.

It is also important to consider carefully the timing of these events. Especially if scheduling something near a major decision by your governing body or the issu-ing of redundancy notices, for example, be aware of unfortunate juxtapositions. Christmas, too, is a particularly difficult time of year if you are in the middle of a change programme. Too much goodwill may come across as hypocritical. While staff having a break from work and from each other may apply to lots of people, if the museum is open over the holiday period, remember not to forget those staff who are working. Wishing everyone a Happy New Year when they return to work is not necessarily the right thing to say, either. So think carefully and plan ahead.

Ensure it is not always senior management taking the lead in being convivial. Give the staff space to breathe and have their usual social gatherings too, without anyone very senior to inhibit conversation.

See also:

35 Keeping up morale during change
40 Internal networks and collaboration

Notes

1 Keynote address, Museums Association Conference, Manchester 2017: youtube/dYQRj1 x7gGY?list=PLYOHZtySwPKQXd0fOfEhuX4v3Wf3Byro_.
2 R. Hewison, J. Holden and S. Jones, *All together: A creative approach to organisational change* (Demos 2010), pp. 71, 99.
3 P.M. Sias and E. Gallagher, 'Developing and maintaining workplace relationships', in R. Morrison and S. Wright (eds.), *Friends and enemies in organisations: A work psychology perspec-tive* (Palgrave Macmillan 2009), pp. 78–100; A. Rzepnikowska-Phillips, 'Conviviality in the workplace: The case of Polish migrant women in Manchester and Barcelona', *Central and Eastern European Migrant Review* (2017), doi.org/10.17467/ceemr.2017.11.
4 R. Hewison, J. Holden and S. Jones, *All together: A creative approach to organisational change* (Demos 2010), p. 99.

42

ACKNOWLEDGING EMOTIONS

> Organizational change produces a cycle of emotions and reactions in people. Staff first felt shock and a sort of numbness, then denial. This moved into anger, and then negotiating and bargaining.
>
> Robert Janes, *Museums and the Paradox of Change*[1]

Emotions will run high at times, especially if staff feel threatened or wish to resist the change, so acknowledging and coping with this is a key part of a leader's job. In Robert Janes' experience, dealing with these emotions, one's own and those of colleagues, is perhaps the most difficult part of the whole change process.[2]

Twenty-first century displays of large-scale emotion are often expressed after the death of a celebrity icon, at the site of a murdered child or after a mass shooting. Mounds of flowers, messages and candles are used to express shared sympathy and horror at what has happened from a world now largely without a strong religious base. So do not try to avoid or discourage emotional reactions; it is entirely natural to show them openly, even if it makes you personally feel uncomfortable.

The importance of emotional engagement in sustaining change

When the Royal Shakespeare Company (RSC) went through several years of major organisational and cultural transformation, a remarkable feature of their leadership and management was the regular and explicit reference to emotions: for change to become embedded, it is not enough to rely simply on logic and analysis – you must acknowledge the emotional impact of the process on the people involved.[3]

The RSC required a set of behaviours to bring about change across the whole organisation, which had been suffering from very low morale, a sort of guiding star by which people could coordinate their individual contributions. These behaviours included:

Altruism – the stronger helping the weaker, not the weaker being choreographed or manipulated to make the stronger look good.

Compassion – engaging with the world and each other, knowing that there may well be mutual pain in doing so.

Tolerance and forgiveness – to allow mistakes and recover from very big mistakes.

Humility – the person who has nothing to learn is incapable of creative dialogue.

Magnanimity – the courage to give away your ideas.

Love – the ability to be inspired by others.

It is unusual to see senior management unafraid to use words like 'love', 'humility' and 'compassion', even in a theatre company. None of these behaviours is inapplicable to museums and galleries. Change will not happen and will not be sustainable without all these elements, because they are about the way people work, what they feel about their work and how they relate to each other. And all of these require putting an understanding of emotions at the centre of organisational change.

Practical tips on how to deal with emotions

All changes arouse emotions, positive as well as negative. If these are not properly managed, the change outcome will be at risk.

Robert Hewison, John Holden and Samuel Jones, *All Together*[4]

As the change leader, if you have your own office, then ensure it is suitable for staff to enter if they are in a heightened emotional state. Make sure your immediate neighbours cannot hear your conversations or peer through a glazed pane in your door and see who is talking to you.

Have a vase of flowers in your office, preferably on a bookcase or a coffee table, to bring colour and freshness to what may be a dull corporate space. It will brighten up the room and soften it with the greenery of nature. Ensure that chairs can be easily rearranged round a coffee table or close together to create a more intimate, safe space for emotionally charged conversations. And always have a box of tissues readily to hand in your office.

If you are based in an open-plan office or can only use a glass-walled room for confidential meetings, it is more difficult to create the right environment. If you are able to, it is worthwhile designating a particular space during a time of major change where any type of confidential conversation can take place, not only with individuals but with unions or smaller groups of staff.

Many of these things are applicable to any leader's office, not only for times of major change.

It is now not only a generalisation but inaccurate to state that female leaders will always have tissues in their office but male leaders can't cope with female staff crying. Coping with a member of staff in tears or visibly upset is not easy for anyone, but if you are a change leader you must be prepared for this and know what to do. Don't be uncomfortable, proffer the tissues, and all you need to say is 'take your time' or reassure them that they do not need to apologise; then don't speak until they do.

Your method of coping will say more about how this makes *you* feel than how the staff member may feel. If you feel out of your depth, then you need to examine your reactions and work on your responses. Leaders should recognise that they themselves will go through a cycle of emotions during a period of change – anger, frustration, hopes and disappointments – that must not be vented on staff.

Sometimes staff members might be tasked with levels of responsibility in the change process which they feel are inappropriate to their professional role and for which they feel unprepared, and trying to sustain the work takes an emotional toll. The converse can also be true: more junior staff looking to make changes might experience strain due to a feeling of lack of agency and support, and this has adverse effects on their morale and wellbeing.[5]

As a staff member who is emotionally stressed, you may not be able to stop yourself filling up or crying. Don't worry. It does not necessarily disadvantage you and it is better to show how strongly you feel than to bottle it up inside. This may also happen during consultation meetings or in discussion with your unions about possible job losses; it may not always be when you are with the Boss. Just be prepared for this to happen to you or to one of your friends or close colleagues. Emotions can take you unawares.

But just as likely as tears are outbursts of anger. Perceived threats to the jobs of close friends, the museum's research and curatorial reputation or its standing in the community may be criticised, and the director as the change leader will be blamed. Again, when it is focussed on you, you are not required to say very much but to listen to the rant and wait until it stops once the ranter is tired. Do not fight anger with anger; you need to cool the temperature and lower your voice. Giving vent to this anger will help the person who has been bottling it up, but it may also give you a valuable insight into their and/or their colleagues' thought processes.

Large-scale change, restructurings and redundancies often create a sense of loss – for colleagues who have left, for former departments and work places or for old ways of working. It is important for leaders to acknowledge that the change process did not appear out of nowhere and that not everything that was done before was bad. Honouring and acknowledging the work of staff and members of the governing body that preceded the change is crucial, and it can make a huge difference to those remaining staff who are still adjusting to the changes (see Chapter 41 on conviviality).[6]

As the title of this chapter states, acknowledge the emotion, do not enter into debates or defence, whatever the emotion on display, and do not take it personally. The emotion is stirred by many different feelings – worry, anger, sadness, loss, professional pride, irritation on behalf of someone else – so do not respond in kind. Keep a cool head but do not appear cold or unmoved by the outbursts of emotion. You can acknowledge it without needing to sympathise.

See also:

20   Building trust
30   Fear of change
35   Keeping up morale during change
46   Avoiding uncomfortable issues
55   Fixing the lessons of change in organisational memory

Notes

1   R.R. Janes, *Museums and the paradox of change: A case study in urgent adaptation* (third edition, Routledge 2013), p. 82.
2   R.R. Janes, *Museums and the paradox of change: A case study in urgent adaptation* (third edition, Routledge 2013), pp. 86–87.
3   R. Hewison, J. Holden and S. Jones, *All together: A creative approach to organisational change* (Demos 2010), pp. 119–20, 137.
4   R. Hewison, J. Holden and S. Jones, *All together: A creative approach to organisational change* (Demos 2010), p. 137.
5   N. Morse and M. McCann, *Becoming a change-maker in museums: Experiences, opportunities and challenges: Reflections on the Museums Association's Transformers Workforce Development Initiative* (University of Leicester 2019), pp. 15–17.
6   G. Anderson, 'Reflections on organizational transformation in the twenty-first century', in R.R. Janes, *Museums and the paradox of change: A case study in urgent adaptation* (third edition, Routledge 2013), p. 201.

PART 5

Why change fails

Across all sectors – business, industry, health and culture – it is widely reported that 70 per cent of attempts at organisational change fail. Those that succeed do so only after about five years.

> I estimate today more than 70 per cent of needed change either fails to be launched, even though some people clearly see the need, fails to be completed even though some people exhaust themselves trying, or finishes over budget, late and with initial aspirations unmet.
>
> John Kotter, *Leading Change*[1]

There are common reasons why most change initiatives fail. Of course, the word 'failure' is absolute, and perhaps not terribly helpful: occasionally a change initiative does, indeed, 'fail' completely, in that it is abandoned; but mostly what tends to happen in practice is that change does not achieve all its aims, is not sustained after the initial push, or goes off at a tangent and becomes something completely different (which is not always a bad thing!).

Part 5 describes the six most common reasons why change 'fails' in museums. If you know in advance what is most likely to go wrong, you can take steps to avoid or mitigate it. These points should particularly be borne in mind as you are tracking and evaluating your change process, which will be covered in Part 6.

Note

1 J.P. Kotter, *Leading Change* (Harvard Business Press 1996), pp. 12–13. Kotter was among the first to cite the 70 per cent figure, which continues to be widely quoted and is backed up by global, multi-industry survey responses, as well as the authors' personal experiences.

43
MISUNDERSTANDING OF CHANGE

The single biggest reason why change fails is that people don't really know what change is. They don't know what to expect, and as a result they don't know what they are signing up for. When it gets hard, seems to take too long or heads off in unexpected directions (as it often does), they panic, or encounter resistance, and often give up.

> 'I don't think we really understood what was meant by organisational change.'
> 'Whenever someone mentions "organisational change" everyone goes "aarggh redundancies, I'm going to lose my job!", and so that sets up a huge amount of resistance.'
>
> Anonymous participants, *Our Museum* programme[1]

What this means is that there is rarely a shared understanding of change across a museum, and that is a recipe for trouble. Often, there is an assumption that change is a single, large, one-off project, focusing on a major, cataclysmic transformation that addresses a particular issue or problem – a short, sharp shock with a discrete beginning and end that potentially impacts everyone's roles and jobs. In reality, change is usually lots of small, incremental changes in different parts of the organisation over a longer period of time, or even continuous adaptation, in which the change process is actually never-ending.

To avoid resistance, misunderstanding and failure, museum leaders should ensure that the motivation for change, and what it might mean for everyone, is widely discussed with all staff and volunteers in the museum as well as external stakeholders.

This will create more buy-in and support and a sense of collective endeavour. It is best to do this *before* the change process starts.

As part of this explanatory process – and probably one of the stages of getting support from the governing body – the director should assess the risks of the change programme overall. If some type or level of 'failure' does ensue, then trustees (or equivalent) would be aware of this risk in advance. They would then be able to support mitigation of the risk too, again ensuring that misunderstanding of the change does not contribute to its complete failure.

See also:

1   What are you changing?
10   Finding common purpose: a shared understanding of change

Note

1   Quoted in S. Ahmad and J. Cummins, *Review of ways of working in Our Museum: Report to the Paul Hamlyn Foundation* (Paul Hamlyn Foundation 2016), pp. 17 and 41.

44

CHANGE IS IMPOSED

> Staff may be resistant to change which they have not been involved in creating.
> Tracy-Ann Smith and Kalliope Fouseki[1]

Change often fails because it is imposed. Imposed change is more of a challenge than more organic or consensual change as the museum has the change dictated by external powers or events. Museum professionals are, in the main, well educated, articulate and opinionated and do not take kindly to imposed change.

In many museums, it is chief executives, directors and governing bodies who decide that change has to happen. Often, they impose a change process without consulting, without explaining what is involved, and, crucially, without acknowledging that they may need to change themselves. They then wonder why everyone is not supporting it – or, worse, actively resisting. At Glenbow Museum, angry staff dismissed the change process as the director's own plan, and expressed hope that his contract would not be renewed so that everything 'could get back to normal'.[2]

In some cases, change is imposed by governments, as evidenced by the increasing political interference in museums and culture by nationalist governments in Europe.[3] In Poland, for example, directors of major museums have been appointed and dismissed on the basis of their political loyalty to a ruling nationalist party rather than their competence, and instructed to change their museum's interpretation to support a narrow government version of history.[4] Often, this change of direction fails spectacularly as museum staff turn against a director who has little experience of managing and implementing change and is merely a figurehead for the government.

Change as a result of global seismic events – terrorism, weather disasters or pandemics – may need to be initially rapid as the impact is likely to be sudden, unexpected and inescapable. Strong leadership is required for the first response in these circumstances, and it is only later on that shared change leadership can be utilised.

In less extreme cases, the imposition of change can be our own fault. We look to leaders to lead change all on their own and to solve all the problems, and sometimes we expect too much of them, blaming them when things go wrong. Governing bodies and directors need to treat staff (and volunteers) as responsible adults, involve them in understanding and managing the change process from the very beginning, and all staff need to assume responsibility for improving things.

Change is not just the director's or someone else's job – it is everyone's job – even when it is imposed and a response to an emergency.

See also:

5   Change is everyone's job
10 Finding common purpose: a shared understanding of change
11 Be open to challenge and new ideas

Notes

1 T.-A. Smith and K. Fouseki, 'Participatory practices in museums: A seismic shift', in K. McSweeney and J. Kavanagh (eds.), *Museum participation: New directions for audience collaboration* (MuseumsEtc 2016), p. 478.

2 R.R. Janes, *Museums and the paradox of change: A case study in urgent adaptation* (third edition, Routledge 2013), p. 85.

3 P. Steel, 'European museum directors warn of "increasing interference" by nationalist governments', museumsassociation.org/museums-journal/news/12062018-european-museum-directors-warn-of-increasing-interference-by-nationalist-governments.

4 On the state of Polish museums, see in general K. Golinowska, 'Between the global, national, and peripheral: The case of art museums in Poland', *Stedelijk Studies* 1 (2014), stedelijkstudies.com/journal/global-national-peripheral-case-art-museums-poland/; P. Piotrowski, *Muzeum krytyczne* (Rebis 2011). For political attempts to influence museum portrayals of Australian history, see K. Goodnow, J. Lohman and J. Bredekamp, *Challenge and transformation: Museums in Cape Town and Sydney* (Berghahn Books 2006), pp. 50–51.

45

RESISTANCE TO CHANGE

> For reasons that have to do with rapid change and the force of habit, we observed that numerous staff were inclined to continue to do what they had done in the past.
>
> Robert Janes, *Museums and the Paradox of Change*[1]

Change can fail because some people resist it: because it is happening too soon or too quickly, or they do not agree with the change or they are afraid of change. Not everyone is persuaded of the need for change at the same time; this is perfectly normal and should be anticipated.

The quotation at the head of this chapter comes from the case study of change at Glenbow Museum: not only did staff carry on as before instead of accepting that they had to work in new ways, but there was a great deal of negativity, constant complaints and hostility within the museum. This professional arrogance caused tensions and problems that were predictable in the face of massive changes and staff reductions, and Glenbow addressed them through a focus on relationships and not just tasks. There are many legitimate reasons to question change and its impact on individuals, which need to be addressed through dialogue and discussion, and not dismissed out of hand. The big lesson is that change has to come from across the organisation; change is everyone's job, even those who are resisters.

But there are also standard excuses that people give for why they cannot or will not change, which have become clichés:

- There's no time, and no resources.
- We did it ten years ago; it didn't work then, so it won't work now.

- We don't do that here.
- It's not what I came into museums to do.
- It's not in my job description.
- I'm a professional, why do I need to change?
- If we do 'x' then we won't be able to do 'y'.

At Glenbow Museum, passive or active resistance to change, especially to new ways of generating revenue, was often rationalised as 'either misplaced altruism or adherence to professional standards'.[2]

A change programme should include anticipating resistance of different kinds, with specific plans to address those challenges. Chapter 31 (Countering resistance to change) focuses on this in more detail as the resistance must be understood if it is to be counteracted, but, broadly, the mechanisms available to change leaders are:

> **Helping staff and volunteers to understand change** by including them in dialogue about the change process.
>
> **Training and support for individuals** with entrenched resistance to change.
>
> **Support for those committed to change**, which creates a group of champions of change across the museum.

In most cases, these approaches will be successful. They are constructive ways of confronting resistance through discussion and development. A disciplinary process, and perhaps ultimately dismissal, should only be used as a last resort once all these other mechanisms have been tried, for individuals who systematically undermine the change process, the work of the museum, and other staff – attitudes that have been described as 'self-serving behaviour' by a leading proponent of change[3] but may more accurately be described as sabotage.

See also:

30 Fear of change
31 Countering resistance to change

Notes

1 R.R. Janes, *Museums and the paradox of change: A case study in urgent adaptation* (third edition, Routledge 2013), p. 63.
2 R.R. Janes, *Museums and the paradox of change: A case study in urgent adaptation* (third edition, Routledge 2013), p. 118.
3 R.R. Janes, *Museums and the paradox of change: A case study in urgent adaptation* (third edition, Routledge 2013), p. 118.

46

AVOIDING UNCOMFORTABLE ISSUES

Change might fail because there are problems inside the museum that are off limits, things that cannot be said, that are too uncomfortable to raise and discuss – and so they do not get discussed. Often, we might blame directors and managers, who do not have answers to some challenges and therefore explicitly avoid them, or lack the self-confidence to have an open and honest conversation the direction of which they cannot control. But sometimes the fear and uncertainty are within ourselves.

> We couldn't learn, we couldn't improve, we couldn't change, because we chose not to speak the truth.
>
> John Holden[1]

Many museums do not have a culture where staff and volunteers feel free to speak openly to managers about problems without fear of being branded disloyal and a troublemaker. This can extend to trustees or external stakeholders, who are often not sure how to raise sensitive topics with museum staff or managers, or often do not understand the museum jargon that professionals use almost unconsciously.

It is not easy to create an environment of trust inside a museum, within which everyone can speak honestly about its work. Two approaches, described in detail in Part 6, can help: reflective practice and the external voice. Both of these are essential tools in a change process, and ideally should be integrated in a robust, formal methodology as part of the way the museum works and learns.

Reflective practice is thinking about and questioning one's actions, being self-critical and constantly learning from what went well, what could have gone better and what might be done differently. It includes the ability to listen, to have an honest dialogue that is about learning, not blame, and being open to challenge, alternative values and working methods.

The external voice is someone from outside the museum who brings a fresh and independent perspective, encourages reflection and helps ensure that difficult subjects are addressed and not avoided. One of the most useful external voices is the critical friend. A critical friend can ask provocative questions, or bring the question into the open that others are avoiding, and ensure that everyone's voice is heard and given value. It is a balance between being positive and constructive, and teasing out the real challenges a museum is facing but may be too nervous to acknowledge.

The authors have encountered directors who see external voices as a threat. In all cases, these were organisations that did not encourage an honest exchange of views, and as a result their change journeys were compromised, because difficult subjects were not being addressed.

Another uncomfortable topic is reporting failure, either failure of the whole change programme or part of it. A director who is the change leader may think 'if I admit this failure to the board, is this a strength; does it demonstrate I have my finger on the pulse of the museum and am perceptive, or is honesty not the best policy here?'

If you are a director using this chapter to help you make this decision, two things will assist you:

- Exactly what has failed and why? (You obviously need to be explicit before you address your governing body.)
- What are you planning to do about it to retrieve/restart/change direction?

The governing body will need to understand what impact this will have on the ultimate goal(s), finances and timetable. If you demonstrate you have learned from the failure, then they will have more faith in your proposed new route or programme if you understand why and how the failure happened.

See also:

11 Be open to challenge and new ideas
51 Reflective practice
52 External voice and critical friends

Note

1 Quoted in P. Bienkowski, 'Why change fails (and what YOU can do about it)', *Journal of Education in Museums* 37 (2017), pp. 18–19.

47

OTHER PRIORITIES

Change can fail because the people involved in it have other priorities, whether strategic, in terms of funding or personal. They focus their time on things which they either think are more important and interesting, or they are involved in too many other projects to be able to focus on organisational change. Reasons for failure include financial problems which require urgent attention either now or to attract funding in the future, or the pressures of the day job.

> The problem was that we treated the change programme like any other project. We worried that it had this disproportionately huge impact on our time and work plans. And, of course, to succeed, it needed to affect everything we do.
> Anonymous participant, *Our Museum* programme

Museum staff are always busy delivering projects funded from many sources, and tend to regard a change programme as just another project in their landscape of projects, which has to be 'fitted in' when time allows. But, of course, organisational change is *not* a project. It is about the way the whole museum works. It is about *how* you carry out all the other projects.

So organisational change should not be treated as a project alongside other projects. Change is holistic and all-encompassing. It affects everything a museum does and how it does it. It is about how it carries out all those other projects.

It is not:

we are doing the following projects — a, b, c, and organisational change.

It is more like:

we are going through a process of organisational change, and meanwhile delivering projects a, b and c, and how we deliver those projects may well have to change as we go along.

Financial priorities

> When leaders fear that money will walk with the people who don't want their traditions disrupted, it can naturally be difficult to commit to the disruption.
> Sarah Lee and Katherine Gean, *The Engagement Revolution*[1]

Change can also fail – or be stopped or held back – when governing boards resist change as a result of worries about its long-term impact on the financial sustainability of the museum, for example in cases where the changes might alienate the current audience or funders and threaten the financial base. The tension between income generation and change was a problem that surfaced in two large-scale programmes in both the UK and the USA, despite their different funding models for museums.[2] In both programmes, the changes were about making community engagement and participation core to the work of the museums (see also Chapters 8 and 25). Boards are legally responsible for financial sustainability, and can be risk averse to making changes that might reduce revenue funding. In the UK, the worry was that participatory work did not generate sufficient income, while in the USA the concern was that diversifying engagement might turn off some subscribers, members and individual donors.

Where these tensions that might threaten change exist, it is vital that, in the first instance, they are brought out into the open and the potential financial implications discussed fully. In any case, a key element of a strategic approach to change is to consider financial implications before you start, and not in the middle of a change programme as a risk-averse reaction when things are getting hard and governing bodies suddenly panic (see Chapter 6: Are you ready for change?). If change is a strategic priority, then ways of resourcing it should be embedded into a business plan at the outset, together with consideration of risk factors. Chapters 8 (Balancing conflicting priorities), 16 (Funding and resourcing change) and 28 (Embracing risk) address these topics and how they can be overcome so as not to disrupt a change programme.

Applying for grants and the impact on long-term change

The way that many museums are funded, in the UK and elsewhere, is either project-funding for delivering pre-defined outputs, or annual or triennial budget rounds which have to be bid for at regular intervals. This leads to constant pressure to report immediate success to funders and so a reluctance to report failure. These time-limited projects keep everyone focused on their delivery targets (see below on the day job), but the grant processes often have long lead times. Longer-term activity is then swallowed up and no real reflection takes place as the finances are used to define success or failure.

Funding from sector bodies such as Arts Council England or Museums Galleries Scotland in the UK, and their equivalents in other countries, has established methods and clear criteria which are published well ahead of the application process. Grants awarded for programmes of work over a three- or four-year period give substantial revenue boosts to museums and allow them to buy in specialist skills for a longer period. As the competition for grants is fierce, a considerable amount of time will be invested in preparing programmes which tick several criteria boxes and deliver significant benefit to the museums. And they will use the skills and knowledge of most of the professional museum staff, from curators and conservators to learning and marketing specialists. In addition, specific one-off grants are regularly available, linked to major anniversaries of events or people, for example, the centenary of the First World War from 2014, so these must also be incorporated into the work flow.

As a consequence of the need for museums to attract revenue funding through projects such as these, there is likely to be a steady stream of grant applications to work on at different times of the year. All this work can not only distract from implementing a change programme but could easily displace it completely. Staff working on these applications often use them as excuses for not attending briefings, consultation meetings or training, so resisters to the change can hide behind what they would refer to as chasing crucial funding.

The change leader and their key implementation staff must guard against this attitude and keep presenting the change as an organisation-wide change programme which may, in the future, affect how grant applications are managed, not the other way round (see Chapter 37). The director must ensure that continuing progress is not diverted by grant chasing, which is yet another distraction that can cause the change to fail.

The day job and change

Change can also be delayed or derailed by staff simply getting on with their day job and using the pressures and demands of this to ignore or block the change programme.

The responsibilities of museum professionals to the public are what drives many individuals, so some staff are likely to argue that the day job should always have priority over everything else. Maintaining events and programmes, advising teachers, servicing school parties, answering public enquiries or mounting and de-rigging temporary exhibitions are all traditional museum services highly valued by the public. So it is easy for some staff to believe that they must focus exclusively on those activities and carry them out in the same way that they have always carried them out, using them as an excuse to not engage fully with the change programme. To carry this belief to its logical conclusion, this can cause the change process to fail, especially if the change is concerned with trying to shift traditional behaviours and ways of working, and how all those traditional museum activities are carried out.

Operational impacts can be difficult to predict even for directors, and leaders of the change could be caught unawares by the impact on staff and on day-to-day delivery of the museum. Those opposing the changes will hide behind their undoubted belief that the day-to-day operation of the museum should always have priority and, perhaps more significantly, display their conviction that change is just another distracting project, not of overwhelming importance for the future of the whole museum. A change leader must be prepared for this.

Continuing to do the day job is important as the public service of the museum must not buckle under the internal pressures of the change programme, so it is an essential part of leadership to ensure that this does not happen. Although it is not a director's role to run the museum on a day-to-day basis (at least in larger museums), it is their responsibility to ensure that the museum keeps operating effectively. With staff not concentrating as normal, and perhaps fear within the organisation, this could be a challenge for a director, who needs to not only hold the ship steady to ensure public service is not affected, but also continue to lead the change programme.

If you are the change leader, you must be prepared for not being able to maintain your usual work routine, as your emphasis will inevitably change. Many people are surprised by the impact on themselves; change is not only about changing staff and the whole organisation's way of working, but you yourself will not be immune. This alone takes energy to process but must not distract you from leadership of the change programme, or it may indeed fail because of this.

Being aware of the likelihood of these reactions can assist you to be prepared to combat them and keep the change programme on track.

See also:

37   Overcoming project mentality

Notes

1 S. Lee and K. Gean, *The Engagement Revolution: A study of strategic organizational transformation in 10 California arts nonprofits* (James Irvine Foundation 2017), p. 58.
2 P. Bienkowski, *No longer us and them: How to change into a participatory museum and gallery – Learning from the Our Museum programme* (Paul Hamlyn Foundation 2016), p. 42; S. Lee and K. Gean, *The Engagement Revolution: A study of strategic organizational transformation in 10 California arts nonprofits* (James Irvine Foundation 2017), pp. 48–50.

48

MUSEUM PROCESSES AS A BARRIER TO CHANGE

All of the first five reasons why change can fail apply to any type of organisation. But museums are different from most other organisations insofar as they have collections that they collect, preserve, document and exhibit, and they actively engage the public with those collections. As a result, all museums have processes around safeguarding collections and making some of them more, and some of them less, accessible to the public. These processes can themselves be a barrier to change.

> [C]urators, registrars, and preparators have long been trained to protect art works and objects from the public, presenting works in ways that keep them separate and safe from visitors. And the curatorial function, in particular, is grounded in the assumption that appreciating and understanding art, and discerning artistic excellence, takes specialized training.
>
> Sarah Lee and Katherine Gean, *The Engagement Revolution*[1]

Museum systems were developed in an era when safeguarding collections by restricting access was the overwhelming priority, hence the specialist, professional guardians of those collections often were, and sometimes still are, formally known as 'keepers'. Traditionally, all decisions about collections, including who had access and who had not, were in the hands of those specialist staff – in many museums, this is still the case. At worst, this can create a 'silo' mind-set, in which collections – including what is collected and how it is documented and interpreted – become virtually inaccessible, even to other museum staff or the director.

However, what communities and funders demand from museums is fast changing, and increasingly museums are responding by encouraging active participation, and sharing collections and knowledge in ways that have an impact on their communities. Yet, it is still the case that processes around collections tend to be overly bureaucratic and opaque. They often deliberately exclude the community voice on the grounds that decisions about collections should ideally be made by museum professionals who understand the needs of a collection and the resources that are required to manage it. Few museums recognise members of the public as a relevant source of expertise, and many judge the public to lack the necessary expertise and objectivity to be helpful participants in collections development.[2] This can be a source of frustration to other staff, volunteers with specialist collections knowledge or to communities.

> The collections are for the public, they should be involved in the decision-making process.
>
> Anonymous museum professional[3]

These processes should be re-examined and adapted to ensure that they are not a barrier to change. This is particularly crucial around who is involved in access, handling, loans, documentation, interpretation, display, acquisition and disposal, to widen the pool beyond specialist curators to include a broader range of staff and community partners (for example, through community panels). Many museum professionals, almost unconsciously, use jargon, acronyms and shorthand when in discussion with their colleagues. This in itself distances the public from the museum staff and creates a mystique around curatorial practice.

To address some of these challenges, a group of California museums and arts organisations changed their structures and individual roles, and deliberately created new paths of internal communication to spread the values of a new way of working. This was achieved through establishing new cross-departmental meetings, and opportunities to discuss the ongoing changes and for collaboration between different teams and departments (see Chapter 10).[4]

Where this has happened successfully, it has involved a museum's human resources department in the discussion about change: as a result, in some museums, not only a diverse range of staff but also community partners are involved in strategic discussions concerning all aspects of managing collections. If a wide range of people are involved, the change programme is more likely to be successful.

See also:

Notes

1 S. Lee and K. Gean, *The Engagement Revolution: A study of strategic organizational transformation in 10 California arts nonprofits* (James Irvine Foundation 2017), p. 51.
2 See H. Fredheim, S. Macdonald and J. Morgan, *Profusion in museums: A report on contemporary collecting and disposal* (Arts and Humanities Research Council/University of York 2018), pp. 40–43, who conclude that none of the museums in their survey held open collections development meetings involving the public.
3 Quoted in H. Fredheim, S. Macdonald and J. Morgan, *Profusion in museums: A report on contemporary collecting and disposal* (Arts and Humanities Research Council/University of York 2018), p. 43.
4 S. Lee and K. Gean, *The Engagement Revolution: A study of strategic organizational transformation in 10 California arts nonprofits* (James Irvine Foundation 2017), p. 51.

PART 6

Evaluating and learning from change

This part describes how to measure whether change is actually happening, what is going well or not so well, and different ways of learning from the process to improve and embed change and to involve external voices in bringing in fresh perspectives. As you track your change journey, you should remain particularly aware of the things that usually go wrong with change programmes, described in Part 5 – this will give you an opportunity to address them before they undermine the whole process.

The thread running through Part 6 is that ongoing evaluation of change should be welcomed as an opportunity for continual learning so that the change can be constantly adapted and embedded successfully. Evaluation of change should ideally be about learning, and not primarily a source for reports or advocacy.

It is important that museums share what they have learned through their change processes, both internally within their own organisations, but also externally, inside and outside the museum sector. Sharing what you have learned, openly and honestly, is an opportunity to reflect further and helps to sustain the change process.

49

TRACKING YOUR CHANGE JOURNEY

> Evaluation has two purposes – one is about proving, the other is about improving. Proving means demonstrating that change is actually taking place. . . .
> When viewed as an *im*-proving exercise, then evaluation needs to be part of a continuous process of learning and growth.
>
> Heritage Lottery Fund[1]

How does a museum know that it is changing in a positive way, and that the change is having the desired impact? The danger is that, over a long-term change programme, it can be easy to lose sight of the original aims and to just carry on doing what you planned regardless, even if the actions are not achieving those aims. To counter this, organisational change benefits from a rigorous and ongoing approach to evaluation, to track where real change is happening within the organisation, where it is not happening, where it might be happening too slowly and if it is happening in the right way. Robust evaluation encourages you to look back and assess your practice, to see if you are heading in the right direction.

Unfortunately, evaluation still tends to have a bit of a bad name – many museums regard it as a necessary evil, as something to be compiled at the end of a project and sent to a funder or stakeholder, typically reporting how brilliantly everything went, admitting no mistakes and registering no useful learning at all. Indeed, a report on museum evaluation found that most evaluations say little that is useful, have little impact, are largely ineffectual, are not taken seriously enough and are not well enough understood by museums, policymakers and funders. It concluded that museums rarely act on the findings of evaluation, and simply see it as part of the chore of accountability to funders, rather than as an opportunity for reflection and learning.[2]

Evaluation should, instead, be welcomed as the ideal mechanism for learning – how else does a museum learn? – and it is absolutely essential if a change programme is to be successful. The function of evaluation is to help the organisation to develop even further: its primary role should not be to 'spin' information for advocacy, funding or public relations purposes, but to help a museum find out what went well, what could have gone better, and what it might do differently as a result of those findings.

> As well as helping to understand more clearly what had gone well and why, evaluation was meant to reveal issues, and show analyses of how individuals and organisations were learning from these changes.
>
> Rachel Moilliet, Tate[3]

The different types of evaluation

Conventionally, museum evaluation is divided into three types: front-end, formative and summative. When evaluating organisational change, these three types can be described in the following ways:

Front-end evaluation is undertaken before a change programme begins, and usually before resources are committed, in order to find out the expectations of visitors, staff and stakeholders and develop the programme to meet those expectations.

Formative evaluation is the process of testing your change programme while it is ongoing. This is particularly valuable, as it helps you to find out what is going well or not so well, and to adapt it as you go along before it is too late to change anything. It also helps you to amend your long-term plan as necessary, if you feel you are not getting to where you want to be, or that the timetable needs to be altered. This type of evaluation is not put on the shelf and forgotten about, like much summative evaluation, but informs the change process.

Summative evaluation occurs at the end of the change programme, and is used to gauge whether you have achieved its aims and objectives.

Often omitted is **baseline evaluation**, which is particularly crucial when measuring organisational change. Baseline evaluation measures where you are starting from, so that you are monitoring your change journey against where your museum was at the beginning of the programme, and not against objective criteria or against other museums. Each museum is unique and sits in a particular geographical, social and financial environment. Each museum's change journey will also be unique: its starting point, the processes it goes through and the length of time it takes will all be different from that of any other museum.

There is a real benefit to starting the evaluation process at the baseline, before the actual change programme starts. It enables everyone involved to agree where the museum is starting from, and to share what it is trying to achieve, what outcomes are being looked for and what change might look like. When undertaking baseline evaluation, it is important to measure the same things you will be measuring later, during the change process. You can then say, 'this is where we were at the beginning of our journey', and it will be possible to look back and say, 'this is how far we have come – this is the progress we made on our journey'.

The most effective way to measure your change journey – and to ensure that you learn and adapt along the way – is to avoid a hard division between front-end, formative and summative evaluation, but, starting with baseline evaluation, run a sort of formative evaluation throughout the whole process, which helps you to learn and to change things as they go along. Ongoing reflective practice is a key part of this monitoring and learning process, and that is covered in detail in Chapter 51. Through ongoing evaluation and reflection, you are constantly measuring your current position against what you hope is your destination.

A clear outcomes and evidence framework

It is useful to develop a clear framework to track your change programme, which will be used throughout the process. This should state what outcomes you are trying to achieve, alongside indicators of success. The indicators of success are how you will track whether or not you are achieving the outcomes – they are the sort of evidence of organisational behaviour you would expect to see if the outcomes were being achieved.

If you are using a change management model (see Chapter 9), you will already have the basic structure of an outcomes and evidence framework. You will have identified your long-term goal and what you need to do to achieve it. One element of a simple Outcomes-Indicators framework for a change programme might look like the example in Table 49.1.[4]

You can also add an intermediate box into the framework, which lists the strategies or actions you will take to achieve that outcome, as in Table 49.2.[5]

TABLE 49.1 An Outcomes-Indicators framework

Outcome	Indicators of success
Communities actively and regularly participate in decision-making about the work of the museum	• Community involvement in governance, shared decision-making and authority, setting targets, monitoring and evaluation • Collaborative exhibition development, including community authoring of proposals

TABLE 49.2 An Outcomes-Strategies-Indicators framework

Outcome	Strategies to achieve outcome	Indicators of success
Staff skills and competencies: shifts in staff capabilities or the museum's staff structure	Create new departments and/or restructure the museum's current departments or job descriptions	All staff roles, responsibilities and relationships reviewed and staff realigned with revised job descriptions
	Improve staff capabilities by providing opportunities for training, learning or collaboration	Proportion of staff who have undertaken training; feedback from staff that they have the right skills for their roles
	Recruit new staff who reflect the diversity of the museum's communities	Composition of board, leadership and staff reflects the cultural and ethnic diversity of the museum's communities

You also need to gather evidence of whether those outcomes are being achieved. It is best to start this process straight away from the baseline evaluation, so that you have a record of your starting point.

Types of evidence to demonstrate change

Evidence of change comes in many forms. The Paul Hamlyn Foundation's major programme, *Our Museum: Communities and Museums as Active Partners*, developed a comprehensive taxonomy of four distinct types of evidence to track change, which involved both museum staff and community partners:[6]

Known and easily shared: this is the sort of evidence that museums regularly collect and disseminate for other purposes, such as annual reports, board/committee reports, vision statements, business plans and visitor profiles.

Known but not necessarily shared: this is evidence that is known but not always written down and shared, such as how values are expressed and made visible, or how experience and learning are shared and passed on within the museum. This evidence might be gathered through questionnaires and interviews.

Emergent or avoided: this is evidence that those involved in the change process might not yet be consciously aware of, or are deliberately avoiding because it is uncomfortable or evidence that is only just beginning to surface. An example might be what happens when there are setbacks, problems, conflicts or challenges, and how these are addressed. Evaluators will usually use observation and nonverbal techniques to surface this kind of evidence. It is a valuable source of learning about change, as it often holds the spark of a new idea or insight, and can shine a light on a difficult barrier, challenge or tension within the museum.

Unexpected discoveries: these are problems, actions, events and consequences that cannot be foreseen at the outset, and one never knows when or where they might emerge. It is useful to record ideas, insights, frustrations and questions as they arise, and share and discuss them within the museum and with evaluators. Such evidence can be very revealing about the change process, and might occasionally lead to the overall plan being amended.

An organisational change process will rarely go completely to plan or smoothly, and the blend of these different types of evidence helps to unearth underlying reasons why things go well or not so well: for example, what happened, how someone got involved in a particular activity, how something came about, who made the decisions and with what assumptions or why a particular event happened at a particular time. There is an enormous amount of learning and insight about change to be gained from gathering and exploring the 'who, what and why?' elements of the process.

The advantage of independent evaluators

Who should carry out the evaluation of a change programme? Many evaluations are undertaken internally by museums themselves. The only advantage is that it is cheaper. The disadvantage is that it is not so easy for internal museum staff to penetrate to the core of a change programme and to be objective and critical about a process that they themselves have been involved in, and perhaps were also responsible for; it also offers a temptation to 'spin' the information in a positive way for advocacy purposes and/or to protect individuals.

The evaluation of a change programme is best led by an independent evaluator, someone who is specifically focused on the work of evaluation and has the time allocated to do the necessary work. The advantages of independent evaluators are that they bring in an external perspective, and have more freedom to raise concerns, ask questions, involve participants, ensure every voice is heard, give constructive critique and encourage ongoing reflection and improvement throughout the change process. External evaluators also bring added value by drawing on their experience of other organisations outside the museum being evaluated.

Of course, it is always possible for a museum to 'spin' the information that it provides to evaluators, to put a more positive gloss on what is happening or has happened. It is up to the evaluator to test and assess the information they are being given, and to probe more deeply. In fact, it is usually in the process of probing that the most useful learning emerges, unearthing the 'who, what and why?' of the change processes, which helps the museum to overcome barriers to change. Clearly, working with an external evaluator can occasionally be an uncomfortable process for museum staff, as it requires openness, honesty, self-criticism and laying bare of museum processes and rationales for decisions and actions – but it is the most effective way of learning what to change and how to change, and reflecting on whether you succeeded.

Involving participants and community partners in evaluation

Not surprisingly, since evaluation is often regarded as a burdensome form of accountability to funders, it is not uncommon for it to be carried out in as short a time as possible as a 'tick-box' exercise by a staff member, or even an external evaluator, in isolation, sometimes after a programme has finished. Increasingly, however, museums are becoming aware of the advantages of involving programme participants and community partners in evaluation.

Circuit, a national programme across the UK aimed at involving young people more directly in galleries, used evaluation to address issues of social justice, democratic participation and organisational change and learning. This involved gallery staff, young people, artists and partners as reflective practitioners, working alongside evaluators and critical friends (see Chapters 51 and 52 for reflective practice and critical friends).[7] Such involvement of all participants in the evaluation process, instead of it being carried out in isolation by staff or by an external evaluator, is a form of 'empowerment evaluation'. This can be defined as 'an evaluation approach that aims to increase the likelihood that programmes will achieve results by increasing the capacity of programme stakeholders to plan, implement and evaluate their own programmes'.[8] It is a way of learning about the real impact of a programme, getting a wide range of perspectives, and encouraging participants' sense of ownership and agency in the museum.

Involving participants and community partners in evaluation does not mean that they take the place of trained professional evaluators. One should not assume that (all) participants and partners have the necessary expertise and critical thinking skills to analyse evidence, produce in-depth results, extract meaningful learning and make recommendations about the impact of change within museums. That is also not their job or responsibility, and in most cases they are interested in being involved in creative forms of data-gathering but not necessarily the subsequent analysis – but involving them in the evaluation process can be of mutual benefit.[9]

See also:

Notes

1   *Evaluating Your HLF Project* (Heritage Lottery Fund 2008), pp. 5–6.
2   M. Davies and C. Heath, *Evaluating evaluation: Increasing the impact of summative evaluation in museums and galleries* (King's College London, November 2013), p. 3.
3   R. Moilliet, 'How can evaluation and reflection become a useful part of everyday work?', in M. Miller, R. Moilliet and E. Daly (eds.), *Circuit – Test, Risk, Change: Young people, youth organisations and galleries working together* (Tate and Paul Hamlyn Foundation 2019), p. 427.
4   Adapted from the outcomes framework of the Paul Hamlyn Foundation programme *Our Museum: Communities and Museums as Active Partners*: see P. Bienkowski, *No longer us and*

them: How to change into a participatory museum and gallery – Learning from the Our Museum programme (Paul Hamlyn Foundation 2016), p. 12.

5 Adapted from the evaluation framework used by the James Irwin Foundation's New California Arts Fund.

6 See S. Medlyn and G. Moriarty, 'Evaluation for change' (2016), ourmuseum.org.uk/ evaluation-for-change.

7 E. Pringle, 'Evaluating "circuit"', in M. Miller, R. Moilliet and E. Daly (eds.), *Circuit – Test, Risk, Change: Young people, youth organisations and galleries working together* (Tate and Paul Hamlyn Foundation 2019), pp. 430–35.

8 A. Wandersman *et al.*, 'The principles of empowerment evaluation', in D. Fetterman and A. Wandersman (eds.), *Empowerment evaluation principles in practice* (Guilford Press 2005), p. 27.

9 See A. Diakopoulou, 'Challenges of the "circuit" evaluation process', in M. Miller, R. Moilliet and E. Daly (eds.), *Circuit – Test, Risk, Change: Young people, youth organisations and galleries working together* (Tate and Paul Hamlyn Foundation 2019), pp. 483–85.

50

THE BENEFITS OF QUALITATIVE
EVALUATION OF CHANGE

> [E]valuation practices that focus exclusively on accountability and value 'objectivity' can attend less to the experience and processes of learning for all those taking part.
>
> Emily Pringle, Tate[1]

Museums are generally expected to deliver to key performance indicators that are about numbers: visitors, events or generated income. They, and their funders and stakeholders, tend to be suspicious of indicators that cannot be measured or counted. They worry that evaluation that is not quantifiable does not constitute proper evidence as it could always appear to be subjective. This is why most evaluation of what museums do is quantitative – something that can easily be analysed and presented in numerical form.

The previous chapter emphasised the importance of a clear evidence framework with outcomes and indicators. But what sort of indicators are we looking for, that will tell us what we need to know? Indicators can tell us certain things, but they only provide an indication that something has happened. They are not proof and there are important things that they cannot tell us, as Table 50.1 indicates.[2]

Indicators can be either quantitative or qualitative. Quantitative indicators help to answer questions about things that are inherently expressed in numbers: how many? how often? how much? But it is difficult for such quantitative indicators to measure how well an organisational change process is going, whether it was successful once it was completed and, crucially, what has been learnt.

If the central purpose of ongoing, formative evaluation of change is not measurement but learning, so that you can constantly adapt, then we need to use

TABLE 50.1 What indicators can and cannot do

What indicators can tell us	What indicators cannot tell us
To what extent the change objectives have been met	Why and how the change programme has made a difference
What progress the change programme has made	Why and how change occurs
The extent to which the targets have been achieved	How communication activities should be undertaken
That the change we are aiming for is happening	Why this particular approach to change has worked

qualitative indicators. Qualitative indicators help to demonstrate, describe or detect that something has happened: *How? When? Who? Where? Which? What? Why?* We saw in the previous chapter that the 'who, what and why?' of the change process yields the most useful learning.

The biggest change programme in the museum sector, the Paul Hamlyn Foundation's *Our Museum: Communities and Museums as Active Partners,* focused on embedding community participation in every aspect of the work of museums, and required changes across whole organisations, from leadership and governance to staff development and external relationships. It concluded that quantitative measures were not particularly useful in evaluating the success of these organisational changes, for example, to show the quality or depth of relationships with the community, and how the museum and community influence each other. Rather, the change journey of the museums in the programme could best be measured qualitatively through three factors:[3]

The response of the community: it was clear that something was going right when community partners publicly advocated the mutual benefits and the impact on their own lives and organisations of partnership work, rather than the museum being its own main advocate.

The organisation's behaviour: an inner confidence not to be driven solely by quantitative measures such as visitor numbers or income, but by the depth of the engagement with the community. It takes confidence in the value and impact of participatory work to make the case to funders and stakeholders that it is of at least equal importance to quantitative indicators of visitors and income.

The impact on individual staff, who felt confident and empowered to do things 'with' not 'to' communities. Confidence and empowerment are intangible and difficult to measure, but are important factors in change.

Qualitative evaluation in practice

The sorts of qualitative questions that need to be asked during a change process, for it to be ultimately successful and sustainable, include: how far have the staff and volunteers bought into the change process? Have they been sufficiently supported?

Do they understand the change? Do they feel listened to? What is staff morale like? Is there resistance to change? Do staff and volunteers trust their leaders and governing body? Has communication of change been effective? Do community partners feel that they have agency in decision-making?

The qualitative tools to evaluate these issues consist of interviews, group discussions, written narratives, oral story-telling, graphic methods, and evaluator observation (which can include observation of body language, and what people don't say as well as what they do say). Of course, some of this can be quantified, by asking respondents to score organisational topics from 1 to 5 – and this is one way of providing what is essentially qualitative data in a numerical format, but it does not have the advantage of offering a response to an open question in a survey or interview, which captures nuances of people's experiences much more effectively.

In our busy lives, the crucial time and space for reflection is often when we move chairs and stick things up on walls, when our hands are too busy to be taking notes. This is one of the reasons why I think journal-keeping is a really important form of documentation for us all.

Roz Hall, *Circuit* programme critical friend[4]

Creative methods for tracking personal and collective change experiences include journals, illustrations and diagrams, games, photography and film, blogs and other online platforms.[5] Increasingly, museums and other organisations are using tools such as the Swedish app Mentimeter to gauge more nuanced responses (Figures 50.1 and 50.2): this is an online collaboration that allows participants to answer and rate questions, provide feedback and vote on preferences anonymously using their smartphones, with the responses visualised in real-time, for example, through word clouds (visual representations of words that give greater prominence to words that are more frequent) or bar charts. Such data can be compared over time to measure progress of aspects such as values, perceptions and behaviours that are key factors in organisational change.

Another effective tool that allows for a sort of visual quantification of qualitative data is a spider graph, commonly used in the health care sector to map the competency of individuals, but also used to rate the performance of an organisation and to map change over time (Figures 50.3 and 50.4). Each axis of the graph represents a question about the work of the organisation (or 'competency'), while the scale on each axis represents the level or rating of that competency. The 'web' of lines linking the axes creates a map of how an individual or organisation are rated, and it can be repeated to create visual tracking of the change process.

Some of the change management models described in Chapter 9 are entirely or partly qualitative, and if you use any of these to plan your change programme then the resulting evaluation will inevitably have a qualitative element. Appreciative

Right now, how much do you endorse the Strategic Direction? ▣ Mentimeter

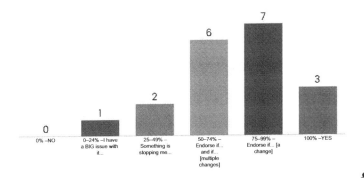

0	1	2	6	7	3
0% –NO	0–24% –I have a BIG issue with it...	25–49% – Something is stopping me...	50–74% – Endorse if... and if... [multiple changes]	75–99% – Endorse if... [a change]	100% –YES

👤 19

Reflect on and rate the following: ▣ Mentimeter

Not at all/Low | I have the support and tools I need to complete my task — 8.7 | Very much so/High

Our long term goal is clear — 8

My stress level — 3.3

👤 3

FIGURES 50.1 AND 50.2 Two examples of using Mentimeter to provide qualitative feed-
back/rating that can be quantified

Inquiry is about having conversations and asking questions, which increases the
capacity within the museum for collaboration and change. This is all qualitative,
not quantitative: it is aspirational, exploring hopes and dreams and a vision of the
changed museum. Similarly, the McKinsey 7S framework includes such qualitative
elements as values, style and skills.

See also:

9   Why modelling change can help

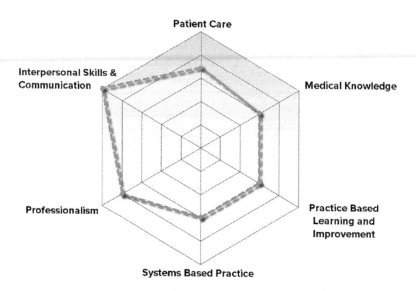

FIGURE 50.3 Spider graph used in health care, mapping an individual's professional competency

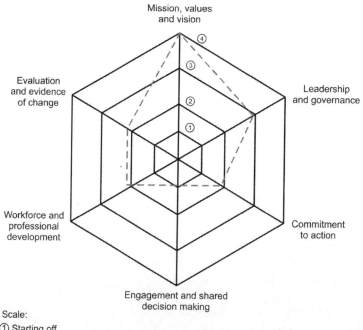

FIGURE 50.4 Spider graph that helps museums self-assess and map their participatory practice

Notes

1 E. Pringle, 'Evaluating "Circuit"', in M. Miller, R. Moilliet and E. Daly (eds.), *Circuit – Test, Risk, Change: Young people, youth organisations and galleries working together* (Tate and Paul Hamlyn Foundation 2019), p. 431.
2 See B. Britton, B. Lipson and Ó. Cronin, *Exploring qualitative approaches to assessing change in organisational development programmes: A 'think piece' commissioned by WWF UK* (WWF UK 2015), p. 33.
3 P. Bienkowski, *Our Museum: What happened next? A review and further learning two years on* (Paul Hamlyn Foundation 2018), pp. 26–27.
4 R. Hall, in M. Miller, R. Moilliet and E. Daly (eds.), *Circuit – Test, Risk, Change: Young people, youth organisations and galleries working together* (Tate and Paul Hamlyn Foundation 2019), p. 478.
5 R. Moilliet *et al.*, 'Creative evaluation methods', in M. Miller, R. Moilliet and E. Daly (eds.), *Circuit – Test, Risk, Change: Young people, youth organisations and galleries working together* (Tate and Paul Hamlyn Foundation 2019), pp. 471–80.

51

REFLECTIVE PRACTICE

> Follow effective action with quiet reflection. From the quiet reflection will come even more effective action.
>
> Peter Drucker, *The Effective Executive in Action*[1]

Reflection is an essential tool in change. It is the process through which a museum learns how to work better, what needs to change and whether the changes it has already made are successful or not. It is the moment of stepping back to see what worked; thinking about and questioning one's actions; being self-critical; and constantly learning from what went well, what could have gone better and what might be done differently. It includes the skill to listen, to have an honest dialogue that is about learning not blame, and being open to challenge, alternative values and working methods.

Ideally, reflection is built into everyday working practices, and involves not only museum staff but external voices such as community partners and other stakeholders. Indeed, one of the first reflective questions to ask is: 'who else should be involved in this discussion so that we capture all perspectives?'

The most successful approaches integrate reflection into regular meeting agendas, providing space to reflect and evaluate together, challenge working practices and help with problem-solving. Some of these can move away from a traditional meeting structure, instead encouraging a more participatory approach by including practical mini-workshops, Open Space and group discussions.

Becoming a more reflective organisation has been a very rewarding part of the work that's been taking place – building in time for discussion, building in time for lessons learned and pushing hard to make sure we take those lessons learned on board and change.

Christine McLellan, Glasgow Museums[2]

However, building reflection into daily practice is still a challenge for many museums, who acknowledge its importance but struggle to find time for it. Yet the common response that it takes time out of normal working is no more than a lame excuse for not doing it: reflection should be central to normal working. Some museum practitioners, when they first try a reflective process, dismiss it as navel-gazing. But to be able to reflect honestly, without assigning blame, and genuinely listen to other perspectives, is a skill to be learned, like any other. It is an essential organisational learning process that feeds back into planning and action, and answers a key question about change: are there things we need to address? It is also an ongoing, iterative process that should not be limited to a discussion at the end of a project.

Too often, museums claim that they do reflect, but admit they have no formal, robust mechanisms for that reflection. In those cases, what tends to happen is that any reflection and learning sits with individuals, is not shared with colleagues and does not influence the learning of the whole museum. For reflection to be effective, it should be formalised into identifiable mechanisms.

The ideal situation is when several processes overlap and encourage continual reflection and learning. Here are some models of reflection that can be built into daily practice.

Set aside five minutes at the end of each meeting to reflect on what just happened: what did you learn; how does it impact the rest of the museum; what could you do differently; was everyone there who should have been there; were there people present who didn't need to be there and/or didn't or couldn't contribute; were all voices heard equally?

Create a regular forum for debate, including staff, community partners and peers from other museums. Use it to bring in new perspectives, share, feedback and reflect on practice. In some organisations, each 'best practice' session has a specific focus, and consists of brainstorming of ideas whose overall aim is to discuss different methods of working tested through various programmes, so that all staff feel confident using them.

Use formal debriefs of projects and programmes – ideally with community partners – to focus on lessons learned and what the museum is trying to achieve.

Use regular meetings with staff and volunteers (i.e. weekly or monthly meetings) to focus not only on operational matters but to include reflection by asking questions and sharing learning: for example, in the last week/month, what went well and what could have gone better? It is important to create an atmosphere that is not about blame but about shared learning.

Empowering staff frees up time for reflection. When staff understand and buy into the strategic aims of the museum, it allows managers to give them more freedom to take decisions within that strategic framework (see Chapter 23: Distributed leadership and sharing decision-making). As a result, meetings no longer need to focus as much on operational details and should become more philosophical and reflective.

See also:

46 Avoiding uncomfortable issues
55 Fixing the lessons of change in organisational memory

Notes

1 P. Drucker, *The effective executive in action* (HarperCollins 2006).
2 Quoted in *Power to the people: A self-assessment framework for participatory practice* (Museums Association 2018), p. 14.

52

EXTERNAL VOICE AND CRITICAL FRIENDS

> A prophet is not without honour except in his own country and in his own house.
>
> Matthew 13:57

A key element in any change process is to include an external voice.

An external voice means involving people from outside the organisation in open and honest conversations about the process of change, in order to bring fresh and independent perspectives to bear, to encourage reflection and to help ensure that difficult topics are addressed and not avoided.

The external voice can come from several sources, including peers, critical friends, funders, evaluators, community partners and artists. Although they all bring different perspectives, each of these external voices offers something specific, and because of that you should have different expectations of their roles. Think about your needs as an organisation and choose the most effective external voice to meet those needs – is it just a talking shop, or will it have a practical application? What is it that a particular external voice can do, and how can it help your museum? External voices are a good way of influencing a governing body, which is often more open to external perspectives about the work of its organisation.

Critical friend: a critical friend is a trusted person outside the museum who takes the time to fully understand the context of the work and the outcomes that the organisation wants to achieve, asks provocative questions, provides additional data, evidence or lessons from elsewhere that give a fresh perspective and offers a critique of work. It is a balance between being positive and constructive, and teasing out the real challenges an organisation is facing. It is about listening to what is said, and what is not said, and being alert to the significance of the body language of the participants, which often can be more revealing than words. Crucially, it is about ensuring that everyone's voice is heard and given value, and that no one dominates a conversation or tries to shut it down.

> It's about the person being able to ask the difficult question, or bring the question into the open that perhaps others are avoiding.
>
> Sally Medlyn[1]

Who can be a critical friend?

In most cases, a critical friend will be commissioned by the organisation to help with a particular piece of work. Although, in principle, peers or community partners can be critical friends, they do need to understand the role and to have the skills and experience to carry it out effectively – and they may be too close to the organisation to be properly objective. In some cases, funders and independent evaluators can also be critical friends, although the relationship with funders can be complex because an organisation may not feel able to be totally honest, as its responses may affect current or future grants. Generally, the most effective critical friends are externally commissioned consultants with a wide experience of different organisations who can take a clear and independent viewpoint to assist you.

Pros

• Is more objective and can help you see things that are hard to see close up.
• Ensures the awkward issues surface and are addressed.
• Ensures everyone's voice is heard.

Cons

• They need time to understand your organisation.
• They cannot effect change, they can only advise, question and prompt.
• If you choose the wrong critical friend, they may be too 'polite' or lack the relevant experience to challenge you effectively.

Peers as external voices – mentoring and sharing

Peers from other museums are an obvious source of an external voice, but generally do not make effective critical friends. The relationship is less about providing structured critique, or even of giving feedback, since often peers can be uncomfortable critiquing each other.

The peer voice is more about mentoring, and the sharing of experience, knowledge, information and learning, or acting as a sounding board: 'we've done this; have you tried that?' It helps if the peers have a shared area of interest and shared goals, and ideally a relationship of trust built up over several years. Unlike the critical friend, this is a two-way relationship, with everyone on the same level.

Peer feedback

Feedback from peers is most effectively done in a structured way. If you want feedback, you need to ask for it explicitly, but for it to work you need to build trust beforehand with a small group which can safely encourage openness.

> London Museum Development currently uses a self-assessment framework with a peer review element. This has operated with success since the South East Area Museums Service developed the idea in the late 1980s.[2] The 'peers' are Museum Development Officers and trained peers from other museums who visit an organisation as part of a structured and supportive process linked to nine organisational characteristics. Their role is to feedback ideas and suggestions from which the organisation can learn.

Pros

- Peers often understand your work and have the expertise to make useful comments. They might, eventually, be very candid, so it can be a very efficient and cost-effective way of learning.

Cons

- Peers often feel constrained from offering proper critique.
- In a peer group, it is important to emphasise that each organisation and its goals are different, so that comparing yourselves against a very different organisation can occasionally feel disheartening.
- It takes time to build trust for effective two-way critique.

Community partners as an external voice – aiding reflection

While it may seem as if community partners could potentially be a good source of critical friends, in practice they can best help an organisation by assisting it to reflect actively and regularly on what has gone well and not so well, on the next steps and on their relationship.

This is quite a different role from that of a critical friend, who is more of an objective facilitator. Indeed, the closer the relationship between an organisation and its community partners, the less able a community partner is to be objective and critical – essentially, and ideally, they become part of the team; but they continue to have a different external perspective which can aid in reflection and bring new thinking, support and problem-solving to a process of organisational change.

> Staff and community partners at Amgueddfa Cymru-National Museum Wales include reflection as the final agenda item at their meetings, to ensure they reflect regularly together on the meeting and the programmes in which they are jointly involved.

Pros

• The views of your community partners are essential if your museum is to be rooted in local needs and stay relevant.
• Museums can act as external voices for community partners too.

Cons

• Their perspectives are crucial, but not as objective as a critical friend might be.
• The longer and closer your relationship becomes, the less objective their perspectives will be.
• Community partners, not being museum specialists, sometimes feel constrained from critiquing a museum.
• Occasionally it takes the input of a critical friend to bring out the voices of community partners on an equal level.

Artists as an external voice – a fresh perspective

Increasing numbers of museums are working with artists, not just to produce new artwork for exhibitions, but for the artist to work with the organisation, to comment on it, and to provide a different perspective from that of museum professionals on how the organisation functions. An artist brings a fresh, creative and open perspective to these issues, unencumbered by layers of professional museum training and history. Often, they can point out working practices which are outdated or illogical, but have been accepted for years as 'the way it is'.

> Glasgow Museums commissioned an artist to act as a catalyst for change within the organisation. The role was to use their practice to help the museum to learn new things about themselves as a community of museum staff, and challenge them to explore new ways of working together as a staff team.[3]

Pros

• Can be a creative and fresh approach to organisational change, re-invigorating the staff.

TABLE 52.1 The roles of different external voices

	Critical friend	Peers	Community partners	Artists	Funders	Evaluators
Teasing out challenges	✓	X	?	X	?	?
Mentoring	X	✓	?	X	X	X
Sharing experiences and learning	X	✓	?	X	X	X
Feedback	✓	✓	✓	X	✓	?
Reflection	✓	?	✓	?	X	?
Fresh perspectives	✓	X	?	✓	X	?

Key:

✓ Yes: this external voice is very suitable for this role.

? In some cases, this external voice might be suitable, but check that the understanding and skills are appropriate.

X No: in most cases, this external voice is not suitable for this role.

- The process can also result in an artistic output, as the artist responds creatively through working with the museum staff.

Cons

- An artist intervention will not appeal to all staff members – some will find it an irrelevant distraction and might respond badly.
- Like critical friends, an artist cannot effect change: they can only challenge and offer fresh perspectives.

Table 52.1 summarises the roles of different external voices.[4]

See also:

11   Be open to challenge and new ideas
25   Community partnerships and change
46   Avoiding uncomfortable issues
53   Learning from peers

Notes

1   G. Moriarty and S. Medlyn, 'Critical friends' (2016), ourmuseum.org.uk/critical-friends/.
2   This was called 'The White Tornado' after a well-known brand of floor cleaner.
3   Glasgow Museums, 'Artists as an external voice' (2016), ourmuseum.org.uk/artists-as-an-external-voice/.
4   From P. Bienkowski, *No longer us and them: How to change into a participatory museum and gallery – Learning from the Our Museum programme* (Paul Hamlyn Foundation 2016), p. 39, based on the experiences of the organisations that took part in the programme *Our Museum: Communities and Museums as Active Partners*.

53

LEARNING FROM PEERS

The phrase 'peer learning' is widely used in the museum sector, and generally understood to be the sort of thing that happens at museum conferences, where colleagues from different organisations share experiences. But it is so much more than that.

It is useful first to ask who our 'peers' in the museum sector are, and what we can learn from them. 'Peers' can be divided into four types, each of which offers different and very distinctive learning about change.

Internal peers

Museums, even relatively small ones, employ people (in both paid and voluntary roles) with a wide range of different skills: not only curatorial and educational, but marketing, design, interpretation, human resources, ICT, managerial, administrative and financial. It is not uncommon for staff and volunteers in individual departments – especially in larger organisations – not to know what their colleagues in other departments really do, and to have no idea at all what knowledge, skills, experience and expertise they have. Yet, many of them – particularly in the non-curatorial departments – will have worked outside the museum sector in diverse environments such as schools and colleges, local and national government and in the private sector. Often, they have previous experience of organisational change, and are a vast, largely untapped resource of learning about a change process and its impact on staff.

A key theme running through this book is that change is everyone's job, and it is useful to acknowledge that all the different forms of expertise across museums bring their own perspectives and understanding of change. Internal discussions about change should explicitly recognise these different types of experience and ensure they are integrated into the debate.

An extremely valuable form of internal peer is the trustee (or equivalent member of a governing body). Best practice in governance should mean that, between them, trustees have a wide range of skills and experience across the whole range of running the museum as a business and a public venue, in addition to its historical and collections content. Often, trustees have worked in the financial, legal, visitor attraction/tourism and educational sectors and bring considerable experience of organisational change. Their experience and learning should be acknowledged and teased out through discussion and debate, not only within the governing body but with staff and volunteers, to contribute to the museum's understanding of change and improve the standard of change management.

Community partners as peers

Ideally, community partners who work with a museum should be regarded as peers and not as outsiders. They bring the skills and experiences of their own environments and workplaces but, as partners, they have also developed an understanding of the challenges facing the museum, and are a valuable source of peer learning.

Many community partners work in community organisations and agencies in the voluntary and charitable sectors. This is a fast-changing sector, always vulnerable to even slight financial and social fluctuations, and so these agencies tend to be extremely adaptable and fleet of foot in how they operate. As a result, community partners often have more experience of organisational change than anyone in the museum. They are used to responding to events rapidly, in more streamlined and less traditional ways, and have much to teach museums about, for example, diversity and up-to-date methods of recruitment, relying more on competency-based frameworks than on formal qualifications such as university degrees. Such approaches are essential if museums are to diversify their staff to better reflect the make-up of their communities.

A good way of sharing this learning is for community partners to deliver training to museum staff, especially on how to work with more diverse audiences, for example, up-skilling staff on awareness of homelessness, unemployment, disabilities, mental health problems or substance misuse. This can have a massive impact on how the organisation is perceived by its communities and can herald a big change all by itself.

Peers in other museums

If your museum is contemplating, planning or already going through a change process, then rest assured: you are not alone! Fortunately, many museums that have trodden the path of change are willing to share their lessons. Some of this learning has been published, especially from larger-scale change programmes that have analysed and reflected on the process. Although this book has incorporated all that learning, it is recommended that those leading change familiarise themselves with the details of the primary case studies.

- The detailed and honest account of the ups and downs of how Glenbow Museum lost 40 per cent of its operating budget and went through a complex process of organisational change, to become the most financially self-sufficient of all the largest museums in Canada.[1]
- The programme *Our Museum: Communities and Museums as Active Partners*, which facilitated organisational change at a number of museums across the UK committed to active partnership with their communities, focusing on learning what worked and what did not.[2]
- The accounts of change at Santa Cruz Museum of Art and History, detailing its remarkable financial turnaround under Nina Simon, building a strong and diverse staff and board, rebuilding the mission and culture of the museum, radically increasing the numbers and broadening the diversity of visitors.[3]
- A short but useful case study of structural change at the Oakland Museum of California, which changed from a traditional hierarchical structure of top-down leadership to one of cross-functional teams that nurtured leadership throughout the entire organisation.[4]
- The *Circuit* programme, which worked with ten galleries across the UK to explore how they could create long-term relationships with youth organisations and young people, and to identify what types of organisational change would be required to make this sustainable. Its publications usefully include the perspectives of diverse participants, inside and outside the galleries, on successes and challenges.[5]
- The New California Arts Fund programme of the James Irvine Foundation, in which ten arts organisations, including museums, set out to make engagement central to all their programming, especially with ethnically diverse and/or low-income communities. Although the programme was more concerned with building capacity for engagement than about wider organisational change, the evaluation had valuable lessons about relationships and partnerships with communities and especially about strategies for dealing with boards that are less committed to change than the staff.[6]

There will be a museum near you that has gone through organisational change. Don't be shy about picking their brains and sharing experiences, and perhaps even setting up a mentoring relationship (see Chapter 52). Contact them, visit them, invite them to give talks to your staff, volunteers and board about their experiences, read their blogs and reports and listen to their conference presentations. The learning will almost certainly be reciprocal. Over the years, the authors have found that museums tend to feel relieved to find out that another organisation has gone through exactly the same problems and challenges that they are facing. So remember, you are not alone: reach out to your peers and share their learning. It will provide you with support, save you a great deal of time and help you to avoid some costly mistakes.

Universities as peers

Departments of museum studies at universities are natural partners and peers for museums, and of course many of their academic staff have worked in a museum at some point in their careers. But the sort of learning they can offer to museums is quite distinctive.

Most of the research that museum studies academics undertake and publish is more theoretical than practical, for example, on wider issues such as social justice, and is often less applicable to the day-to-day life of people who work in museums. Robert Janes accuses museum studies departments of being 'insular' and not caring about what is actually happening in contemporary museums.[7] In fact, they are probably more interested in global topics rather than the intricacies of museum management and change. However, they can be interested in longer-term research on museum programmes – across one museum or a group of organisations – especially if there is potential for learning that is innovative, transformative, has lessons for the museum sector as a whole and has wider societal impact.[8] Universities without a museum studies department may be potential peers if they have an anthropological interest in change, especially in the cultural sector as a whole. Some university anthropologists specialise in museums, employing methods of ethnographic fieldwork and participant observation within museums to explore how they function as producers of public culture.[9]

Several university museum studies departments also run research centres that carry out action research with museums and other cultural organisations, often concerned with change, experimentation, the value of museums and culture, audience attitudes, diversity and health and wellbeing.[10]

University museum academics can therefore offer different perspectives on a museum's change programme or its wider work, often placing it within a wider societal context, and asking challenging questions about why you are doing what you are doing.

See also:

11 Be open to challenge and new ideas
24 Involving stakeholders in the change process
25 Community partnerships and change

Notes

1 R.R. Janes, *Museums and the paradox of change: A case study in urgent adaptation* (third edition, Routledge 2013).

2 P. Bienkowski, *No longer us and them: How to change into a participatory museum and gallery – Learning from the Our Museum programme* (Paul Hamlyn Foundation 2016); *Our Museum: What happened next? A review and further learning two years on* (Paul Hamlyn Foundation 2018); and the web resource ourmuseum.org.uk.

3 G. Dunn, 'How Nina Simon reinvented Santa Cruz art', *Good Times* (Santa Cruz), 4 June 2019, goodtimes.sc/cover-stories/nina-simon-reinvented-art-santa-cruz/. See also N. Simon, *The art of relevance* (Museum 2.0 2016).

4 G. Anderson, 'Reflections on organizational transformation in the twenty-first century', in R.R. Janes, *Museums and the paradox of change: A case study in urgent adaptation* (third edition, Routledge 2013), pp. 192–204.

5 M. Miller, R. Moilliet and E. Daly (eds.), *Circuit – Test, Risk, Change: Young people, youth organisations and galleries working together* (Tate and Paul Hamlyn Foundation 2019); M. Miller, R. Moilliet and N. Jones, *Circuit - Test, Risk, Change* (Tate and Paul Hamlyn Foundation 2017).

6 S. Lee and K. Gean, *The Engagement Revolution: A study of strategic organizational transformation in 10 California arts nonprofits* (James Irvine Foundation 2017).

7 R.R. Janes, *Museums and the paradox of change: A case study in urgent adaptation* (third edition, Routledge 2013), p. 364.

8 E.g. R. Sandell, *Museums, moralities and human rights* (Routledge 2016).

9 E.g. S. Macdonald, *Behind the scenes at the Science Museum* (Berg Publishers 2002); *Memorylands: Heritage and identity in Europe today* (Routledge 2013).

10 E.g. the Research Centre for Museums and Galleries at the University of Leicester.

54

LEARNING FROM OTHER SECTORS

The previous chapter was about learning from the experiences of change of peers in the museum sector. But other sectors – especially the wider cultural sector, business and health – have considerable experience of change too; often, perhaps, more direct experience than the average museum. They have identified many of the same challenges as museums face: after all, most organisations that have gone through successful change have an effective change leader, a sense of common purpose, staff buy-in and have overcome resistance to change, which is exactly what museums face. It is worth learning from the solutions that these other sectors have found, rather than struggling to reinvent the wheel.

There are two ways of learning from other sectors. One is by finding a mentor from another sector who has direct experience of leading change; the second is by studying the lessons of change published by other sectors. These two methods may be complementary rather than interchangeable.

Mentoring from outside the museum sector

By far the best way to learn from the experience of change of another sector is to learn directly from someone who has led successful change. And the best way to learn is to have such a person as a mentor through your change process, someone who will share their experiences of change with you and provide regular support, feedback, practical tips, an external perspective, help with pitfalls to avoid and with problem-solving, and who will also challenge you to think innovatively and possibly outside your comfort zone.

A good local source of business mentors is a chamber of commerce, a form of local business network found all over the world. Many countries also have specific organisations that act as a bridge between the business and arts sectors, and which broker appropriate mentoring relationships. For example, there are independent

Arts and Business teams for England, Scotland, Wales and Northern Ireland; Americans for the Arts in the USA; Business/Arts in Canada; and Creative Partnerships Australia. The role of these bridge organisations is to broker and strengthen partnerships between business and arts organisations, to source business people for the boards of arts organisations and to host events at which arts and business professionals can meet to exchange ideas, address challenges and share best practices. Although some museum professionals may consider their members too commercially minded, many museums lack business skills.

To ensure a beneficial mentoring relationship, both parties must have a clear understanding of the process and shared expectations of the relationship, for example, how often you meet, what sort of support and advice you might expect and a mutual commitment to confidentiality.

Lessons from other sectors

Learning from the experiences of change of other areas of the cultural sector is useful, as there is often overlap with the activities (and values) of museums, and so their lessons can be particularly relevant. The most insightful report on change in the cultural sector is that on the **Royal Shakespeare Company** (RSC), already cited elsewhere in this book.[1]

The RSC had embarked on a three-year programme of change in the way it was led and managed. The change journey was followed by the think tank Demos, which observed the process and published its findings. Most of these are applicable to other cultural organisations, including museums.

- Change is a continuous process, not one event.
- Internal change has to align with external conditions: there needs to be a common understanding of external expectations of the organisation.
- Leaders are at the heart of a network, not at the top of a pyramid.
- The importance of acknowledging emotions that are a major feature of organisational life, but are often ignored, and even more rarely expressed, by leaders.
- Creativity – and museums are just as much creative places as theatres – depends on collaboration, which needs to be facilitated through good communication and shared norms of values, behaviours, responsibility, honesty and trust that enable people to work together instead of being micromanaged. This building of the organisation as a community is the key to successful experimentation and innovation.

Health and care sector

One of the most progressive sectors globally in terms of organisational change is health and care. The language in this sector is often about 'transformational change', which requires a fundamental rethink to create an entirely new and more effective way of addressing problems. The King's Fund researched four case studies of innovative and successful transformation at health and care sites in England and the Netherlands, and drew out common lessons about how and why transformative change succeeds.[2] These lessons are also relevant to museums, and echo many of the points discussed throughout this book.

> [T]ransformation is multi-layered, messy, fluid and emergent. It is not merely about changing how a service operates. . . . It requires a shift in the power balance within relationships, in mindsets and in ways of working, at every level of a system.
>
> Durka Dougall, Matthew Lewis and Shilpa Ross,
> *Transformational Change in Health and Care*[3]

Its report argues that transformational change is best created 'from within', not externally imposed. For change to be embedded and successful, it is ideally led by frontline staff and service users, and requires collaborative and distributed styles of working and leadership (cf. the RSC report cited earlier). As in the museum sector, one of the main challenges is a sense of inertia and preservation of the status quo. The case studies give similar examples to those found in many museums of 'old' power (held by a few, closely guarded and inaccessible) colliding with 'new' power (enabled by people at grassroots level who have agency, open and shared). But there were also examples of old power enabling new power, where leaders recognised the need to allow the community to co-design programmes. Indeed, the case studies are evidence of the power of communities to drive change and provide ideas that completely re-shape health care provision – a participatory trend that is also apparent in museums.[4]

The case studies underline the importance of giving staff time and space to understand change and to be able to lead it, and to offer support, through training, coaching and organisational culture, instead of demanding delivery of change with no time to prepare or engage. A particularly useful insight is the importance of identifying 'invisible' forces, such as the impact of physical spaces and personal contact on feeling valued and healthy, the impact of job titles to empower or disempower, and the diversity of attitudes and preferences across staff. These forces can be both invisible and impassable, and can derail transformational change programmes or create new problems and resistance unless they are identified early on and addressed, for example, through regular reflective practice (see Chapter 51).

The health and care sector is also an inspiring example of how to be open to learning about the latest change thinking and practice from around the world, and translating it into innovative, practical approaches to change. In the UK, some museums and heritage organisations have learned about new ways of implementing change through informal partnerships with Horizons, a team within NHS England that supports leaders and staff to think differently about large-scale change and accelerate it, effectively nurturing change agents throughout the health and care system.[5] These sorts of bodies are another potential source of mentors and advice from outside the museum sector.

See also:

7   What is your stimulus for change?
10 Finding common purpose: a shared understanding of change
23 Distributed leadership and sharing decision-making
34 Champions of change

Notes

1 R. Hewison, J. Holden and S. Jones, *All together: A creative approach to organisational change* (Demos 2010).
2 D. Dougall, M. Lewis and S. Ross, *Transformational change in health and care: Reports from the field* (The King's Fund 2018).
3 D. Dougall, M. Lewis and S. Ross, *Transformational change in health and care: Reports from the field* (The King's Fund 2018), p. 84.
4 See the examples from around the world in K. McSweeney and J. Kavanagh (eds.), *Museum participation: New directions for audience collaboration* (MuseumsEtc 2016).
5 nhshorizons.com.

55

FIXING THE LESSONS OF CHANGE IN ORGANISATIONAL MEMORY

So far, Part 6 has dealt with how to evaluate change and learn from it, so that the change is continuously adapted, embedded and sustained. A crucial element in sustaining change is to ensure that the major lessons are firmly embedded in the organisation's memory. A process of change can take years and be very disruptive, so it is important that all those involved – including new staff who were not there at the start – retain a clear understanding of how it all began and why, what the organisation has learned, how it got to here from there, and where it is heading.

Yet, museums are often very bad at organisational memory. For organisations which deal in people's memories and stories, this is an often surprising failing. It is not easy to achieve and is made more difficult in an environment of funding cuts and staff changes, as people move on or are reassigned, and roles are restructured. This is particularly the case within local authorities, where museum specialists might suddenly find themselves managing other cultural services, markets and cemeteries or being the client for externally managed sports and leisure activities.

> People will default to what's old and comfortable.
>
> **Anonymous arts manager[1]**

Change processes exacerbate this organisational forgetting. Since change is often imposed from the top, it is governing bodies and senior managers who make decisions, excluding staff and volunteers (and often also stakeholders and partners), and they do not necessarily communicate what they have decided, why, and what is happening. There is a danger that everyone else feels confused or, worse, disempowered and disengaged. Furthermore, change programmes often involve secondments or staff on temporary contracts, and there is a lack of mechanisms to ensure that their learning and experiences are recorded and shared; or some staff revert to old attitudes and practices once the formal change programme is ended, owing to the lack of mechanisms for fixing the lessons of change, and ensuring the culture stays changed.

The challenge is essentially how to transmit learning within the museum over a long period, so that it sits within the whole organisation and not with one particular staff member (whose learning is lost when they leave). The authors have been in the position, as external consultants on change programmes, of being the effective keepers of an organisation's memory. New staff have called on us to find out what the organisation originally committed to, why decisions were made, who by and in what circumstances, and have even requested original documents, policies and strategies that the staff themselves cannot track down or access. Remarkably, some museums do not have systems whereby documentation is made available and accessible to new staff – instead, documents are locked in computers or behind passwords of departed staff. As the author's careers have spanned huge technological change – from electric typewriters to networked computers and laptops for home working – this problem is often an accident of outdated inaccessible technology rather than a deliberate policy of forgetting the past. But the result is that much information is effectively lost to organisational memory.

There are three ways through which organisational memory can be preserved and as a result contribute to continuing change:

- Embedding the learning within the whole organisation.
- Keeping the change process under review.
- Building on the learning for the next stage of the journey.

Embedding the learning across the museum

> If staff leave when a project ends, build in ways to ensure what was learned from a project stays within the institution.
>
> Mark Miller, Rachel Moilliet and Nicole Jones, *Circuit*[2]

'Organisational memory' means just that: it is the memory, experience and learning of the whole organisation, and not of one individual staff member or volunteer, or of a group of senior managers or a governing body. It is memory, learning and experiences that can be passed on to future generations of the organisation. Other chapters in Part 6 cover some ways in which learning from change can be shared across the whole museum, through ongoing evaluation and reflective practice that involve all staff and volunteers (see Chapters 49, 50, 51 and 56).

It is the role of written policies and strategies, as well as business plans and annual reports, to embed aspirational and actual change into the day-to-day working of the museum, and sustain the change by committing it to organisational memory. They are the sort of 'instrumental' change that helps with staff buy-in and allocation of resources.

The language used in policy and organisational documents is important and revealing about where the museum sees itself. For example, an analysis of the language of such documents from a group of museums, exploring their institutional attitude to engagement and participation, found that community members were too often cast as beneficiaries or 'supplicants' on the periphery, with senior managers and staff as 'carers' in the centre.[3] This imbalance of power was subtly replicated in the wording of policy documents, revealing an underlying philanthropic but patronising bias, using phrases such as 'we have a responsibility' and 'we can make people's lives better', and words like 'provide' and 'tell', rather than more inclusive and collaborative language. It is a useful reminder for those writing strategy and policy to think carefully about the words they are using, how they reflect the change that the museum is aspiring to, and the assumptions behind and implications of wording. Careful attention to language is necessary to ensure that the changed museum is not simply rhetoric but a reality, and brings the new vision into line with its values.

Ideally, such strategic documents should always be produced collaboratively, ensuring maximum understanding and buy-in from staff, volunteers and community partners – rather than, as too often happens, being written in isolation by a senior manager to a tight deadline. A collaborative approach reinforces the input and role of staff champions of change and brings new staff on board.

No strategic document should stand alone; it should be part of a web of instrumental policies, best implemented through other strategies, aligned to the overall corporate vision and mission, and ratified by the governing body. This gives authority to the strategy and potentially unlocks resources, impacting the work of the whole museum.

Such documents – particularly annual reports and business plans that can show progression over a period of time and so are a good tracker of a long-term change programme – are not just a form of accountability or advocacy, but should be a guide to working practices and a record of the organisation's memory. As such, they should not just sit on websites or on shared drives or intranets, but be part of induction packages for new staff, governing body members and stakeholders, so that they can understand why the organisation is where it is and assist with the continuing work of adapting, embedding and sustaining change.

The authors have both worked in historic museums founded in the nineteenth century where staff induction did not include the history of the museum itself. Particularly if you are a leader, knowing your predecessors and their contribution to the museum's development (for good or ill) can be crucial in understanding how the museum came to be as it is today.

Reviewing change and creating the 'new normal'

> There can be no return to normal because normal was the problem in the first place.
>
> Graffiti in Hong Kong during the Covid-19 pandemic, 2020

Museums should ensure that the new habits of behaviour, new models and new policy objectives are kept under review. This is about building the 'new normal', that is, patterns of behaviour that will eventually become an embedded element of the organisational culture (see also Chapter 50 on qualitative evaluation of change).

In practice, this is likely to take time and reiteration to fully embed even the most successful bits of learning. It may be useful to design and implement an explicit review process. What this looks like and how regular it is will vary according to the size and scale of the museum and of the change it is aspiring to achieve. This review may be linked to the change management model chosen at the start (see Chapter 9).

Building on the learning

Arguably, change never stops (see Chapter 2), or should never stop. Whatever your museum is changing, the funding, political and social environment around you will also continue to change, which will probably require further change from you, and so the cycle goes on. You will always be in the position of having to identify new or revised priorities for the next phase of the museum's journey. These new strategic objectives for the next phase of change will be based, partly or entirely, on what you have already learned through the change process. In this way, learning from change is embedded in the museum's continuing development and becomes part of its organisational memory.

This might mean, for example, extending new models of partnership into other aspects of the museum's work; taking imaginative new risks with collaboration and engagement; building on pilot projects you have tried or extending your commercial activities. Whatever your next steps, make sure that you extract as much learning as you can from your change process using the approaches described here in Part 6, and explicitly embed it within the routine and regular process of refreshing and revising the strategic, business or service plans. In this way, the learning from change will always inform your future development, and no staff or volunteers will ever wonder why they do things the way they do.

See also:

21 How to sustain change
39 Communicating change, internally and externally

Notes

1 Quoted in S. Lee and K. Gean, *The Engagement Revolution: A study of strategic organizational transformation in 10 California arts nonprofits* (James Irvine Foundation 2017), p. 47.
2 M. Miller, R. Moilliett and N. Jones, *Circuit – Test, Risk, Change* (Tate and Paul Hamlyn Foundation 2017), p. 49.
3 B. Lynch, *Whose cake is it anyway? A collaborative investigation into engagement and participation in 12 museums and galleries in the UK* (Paul Hamlyn Foundation 2011), pp. 15–16.

56

SHARING THE LEARNING

> [I]t is important to remain open to the scrutiny of colleagues and welcome them into your organization, even during intensely difficult times.
> Robert Janes, *Museums and the Paradox of Change*[1]

Part 6 has covered different ways of learning the lessons of change, through reflective practice, critical friends and other external voices, and from peers and other sectors. It is important that museums share what they have learned through their change journeys, both internally within their own organisations, and externally, inside and outside the museum sector. Sharing what you have learned is an opportunity to reflect further on your own learning, stimulate debate and dialogue, find out about other approaches to change, challenges and solutions, and to 'benefit from the thoughts and impressions of outside observers'.[2] It is also an opportunity to help others, who may be grappling with similar challenges in their own organisations.

Sharing openly and honestly

Sharing good practice and knowledge is something all museums should always do, but it will only make a difference and be worthwhile if they are prepared to be honest about what actually happened: about what went well, what could have gone better, and what failed completely. Everyone – individuals and organisations – learns more from mistakes than from things that went perfectly.

> It was important to avoid a tendency to want to share only positive outcomes and gloss over what might be considered a failure.
>
> Rachel Moilliet, Tate[3]

Understandably, many museums tend to be cautious about sharing 'failure' or what did not go so well, and there are good reasons for this. Among them is concern that funders and stakeholders might lose confidence if things are perceived not to be going well, and as a result withdraw or reduce funding and support. Bad publicity and negative coverage of problems by the media are also a problem, as the media is now always well informed about the complex situation of museum funding and varieties of governance. This is particularly sensitive for local authority museums that are funded from local taxes, and therefore need to demonstrate that the money is being used judiciously, not frittered away on wild experimentation with little benefit for the community. There is also a sense of competition between museums for funding, and the fear of appearing inadequate or, worse, incompetent in the eyes of colleagues.[4]

In some cases, though, reluctance to talk about mistakes can be a symptom of an organisational blame culture. It is still the case that, rather than be honest about what did not go as well as it could have done, many museums go into knee-jerk 'advocacy mode', overclaiming successes and underplaying problems.

Mistakes are, however, a normal part of professional life and should be accepted as such. They happen all the time. A mistake is simply an event, action, judgment or decision that creates an undesired or unintended outcome, and many mistakes can be traced back to faulty or over-optimistic assumptions or errors in decision-making. An important element of everyone in the museum taking responsibility for their work and for their role in change is to be willing to put their hands up when things go wrong and admit 'I should have done this or that'. That is how the whole museum can learn: through everyone talking about it and sharing, the whole organisation – and other organisations too – can learn at the same time, even from one single mistake.

Increasingly, funders are understanding how museums learn and grow, and many of them are interested in how those organisations change as a result of the funding rather than just focusing on quantifiable outputs such as numbers of events and visitors or a completed capital project. The wisest are urging museums and others to be open and honest about things that did not go so well, and to demonstrate that they have identified them and learned from them. This learning from mistakes is one of the keys to successful change – and sharing that learning will be to the benefit of the whole museum sector.

There are various ways to share learning, and different audiences for that sharing.

Sharing learning internally

This is not just one-way communication from a director or manager about what is happening in the change programme, but genuine internal sharing and discussion involving all staff and volunteers in the museum about what is going well and what could be better. It is important to create an open and honest atmosphere of trust that is about shared learning, not blame. Some of the ways in which this can be done have been suggested in Chapters 5 and 51:

Create a regular forum for debate as a way to track the learning from change.

Organisational reflection through facilitated mini-workshops or Open Space discussion, focusing on learning from change, in which the agenda is created by the attendees rather than imposed by managers.

Action learning sets that divide staff and volunteers into groups of between five and seven who meet regularly to address practical issues and support their own learning and development. This might particularly relate to how the learning from change affects roles and behaviours and how it can be applied to their needs and challenges.

Use regular weekly or monthly meetings to identify challenges and share learning by incorporating a discussion or workshop element.

Q&A sessions after all-staff presentations on the change process by leaders.

Design continuing professional development programmes to incorporate the learning from change, especially around cultural and behavioural change (see Chapters 19 and 33).

Draw in a wider range of staff and volunteers to participate in practical aspects of the change programme, exposing them to new ways of thinking and working.

Sharing learning with the wider museum sector

There are obvious mechanisms for sharing within the museum sector, such as annual conferences or regional workshops, at which organisations and individuals can propose sessions to present and discuss significant work they have been doing. Probably the most useful approach is to consider who you want to share with and at what level: whether the audience for your sharing – and the audience that will give you the most useful feedback – is local, regional, national or international, or a mix of all four. It may well be that you feel your change programme is so innovative and on such a grand scale that it is internationally significant, and sharing it is an opportunity for international advocacy and impact; but it is also true that, often, the most useful and considered feedback comes from more local and regional colleagues who really know your organisation, your environment and your communities.

Local mechanisms for sharing include organising seminars or workshops to 'showcase' and discuss your change programme with other local museums, especially if there is a shared ambition to make an impact within a local area. Another traditional method, of course, is the museum annual report, which can report on change and future ambitions – although now it sits on a webpage and is in theory available to everyone, the sad truth is that for most museums its audience is primarily local stakeholders and funders.

At a **regional** level, in the UK, regionally based museum development officers organise regular events and training, which bring together individuals and organisations to share and learn how to improve practice. Similarly, in the USA, although the 'region' is considerably larger, the American Alliance of Museums has six regional associations which hold their own conferences and events. National and regional museum federations in the UK are sadly not as active or well supported in some areas as they once were; many museum professionals find it difficult to leave their museums to even attend formal training.

Nationally, in the UK, many national museum bodies hold major annual or biennial conferences, usually over several days, which are ideal opportunities for showcasing and discussing change, often as part of themed sessions: for example, the Museums Association, the Association of Independent Museums, Museums Galleries Scotland and the Welsh Federation, and there are conferences for different museum disciplines, for example, the Group for Education in Museums and the Social History Curators' Group, both of which in recent years have held annual conferences devoted to change. Similarly, the American Alliance of Museums and most countries' national museum associations hold annual meetings which are all about sharing and learning. Janes is disparaging about museum conferences, calling them 'devoid of new insights and uninspired', but, while all of us have endured such events, in recent years many have pioneered innovative formats and addressed controversial and challenging topics.[5]

Many major national conferences have an **international** reach. An explicitly international body is MuseumNext, founded in 2009 specifically to explore what's next for museums and to discuss change in the sector. This holds conferences in cities all over the world, each with a specific focus. There are also real or online museum networks in which participants share and discuss their issues, for example NEMO – the Network of European Museum Organisations – which also has its own annual conference, or various museum-related discussion groups on online professional networking sites such as LinkedIn.

In principle, a museum website should be an excellent medium for sharing the lessons of change. In practice, most institutional websites are used primarily for advocacy and information for visitors, with strict control over who is allowed to speak for the 'brand' and central editing of content, rather than encouraging the sharing of lessons and mistakes. Perhaps a more effective way of sharing internationally online is to write a blog about your change process. Unfortunately, the vast majority of these only reach small audiences. However, by sharing the lessons of your change programme with influential bloggers, such as Nina Simon's Museum 2.0 blog, you can reach a huge international audience.

Some larger-scale change programmes, or the peer networks mentioned below, run across several museums and have created bespoke websites explicitly to host blogs and encourage the sharing of opinions, successes and mistakes. These are not without problems: occasionally, they are restricted to programme participants, and so the 'sharing' is limited; and, when they are accessible to all, some participants feel constrained from being open and honest in a public space. But they can work as a shared reflective space, provide different perspectives on similar topics, and function as an archive of learning that is not necessarily centrally controlled and ratified.[6]

Of course, you may wish to discuss your change programme with museum colleagues more confidentially, especially if it is still in progress and you have difficult or controversial matters to consider. A good and safe approach is to bring together a small group of colleagues, whose opinions and experience you respect, in a workshop under the so-called Chatham House Rule, designed to increase openness of discussion while protecting confidentiality.[7] Such discussions with trusted colleagues are an excellent way to discuss difficult issues, while ensuring that they stay within the room.

Peer networks: in recent years, various developmental groups have used this model and have made a significant impact on innovative leadership within the UK museum sector. The *Clore Leadership* and *Oxford Cultural Leaders* both recruit from across the cultural sector and not simply museums, and together with *Museums Resilience Leadership*, led by the Black Country Living Museum, and *Transformers*, run by the Museums Association, they all aim to encourage more effective change leadership and innovative practice. They also encourage each cohort to build upon friendships created at their residential sessions and sustain them through peer networks afterwards to support change beyond the formal courses. These form confidential, safe and supportive fora to share experiences and learning and provide personal support for sometimes less experienced leaders. A similar international peer network is Of/By/For All, which helps connect cultural organisations with their communities in effective ways.[8]

In the UK, groups such as Directing Change (founded in 1990) and Women Leaders in Museums Network (since 2006) are examples of well-established, self-governing and self-determined networks. They provide support and friendship around leadership and change and can provide a model for others to follow. Museum Hue in the USA and Museum Detox in the UK are networks for people of colour who work in the museum, heritage and cultural sectors. They are particularly interested in transformational change in museums that addresses issues of diversity and equality.

Sharing learning beyond the museum sector

Chapter 54 showed that museums can learn a lot about different approaches to change from other sectors. Similarly, as museums go through the process of change, they too will generate learning that is useful to organisations beyond the museum sector. Some of these may be actual or potential strategic partners, with whom sharing learning about change may develop into or cement a relationship.

These other sectors fall into one of four groups:

Analogous sectors, such as the performing arts, heritage, libraries, archives, and science and discovery centres. Often, these have similar approaches and challenges to museums – they all tend to have collections of some kind and engage with the public to share those collections and knowledge – and much of the learning about change is transferable. For example, the learning about change and participatory practice from the Paul Hamlyn Foundation programme *Our Museum: Communities and Museums as Active Partners* (see ourmuseum.org.uk) has been used successfully in all of these sectors, not only in the UK but across Europe.

Voluntary and charity sector agencies often work with museums at a local level, and are a good source of strategic community partners. These can cover volunteering, unemployment, diversity, substance addiction, homelessness, refugees and migrants, among many others. In general, such organisations have to be very adaptable to a fast-changing economic and social environment, and are always interested in lessons about change, especially from local organisations, such as museums, which have an impact on the clients and networks of those agencies.

Sectors in the forefront of radical change, which include health, international development and change managers, are always open to different approaches to change. This is especially so for organisations, like museums, whose change processes can directly affect and involve the public and communities, and so have a wider societal impact (see Chapter 54).

Within **local authorities**, especially in the UK but also across parts of Europe, increasingly museums are parts of broader departments of arts and culture, leisure, community development, wellbeing and education. The lessons of change can be relevant to a whole department, and not only to the museum, particularly in the face of frequent local authority restructuring which has become a standard response to financial pressures. Also, it is likely that you may not be able to integrate and sustain some of the changes you want to, unless the whole wider directorate – or even the whole local authority – embraces and adopts them.

You may already be working with some of these sectors, in which case it is relatively straightforward to organise joint workshops or seminars to share lessons about change, with, for example, your existing community partners in local voluntary or charity sector agencies. You could offer a talk, or even offer to train their staff and volunteers on aspects where your museum has greater expertise. Sharing learning about change through cross-departmental training is also a useful approach within local authorities.

With other sectors, it is often a case of reaching out to organisations and working in partnership to develop and run conferences, seminars or training about different approaches to change. Rather than restricting yourself to the usual annual museum conference, offer a session to a conference in another sector, to share (and learn about) different approaches to change. University departments of museum studies or arts management, policy and practice are another good source of partners with whom to share – they will often be interested in organising seminars about change, and integrating the lessons of your change programme into their own research and advisory work. Many outside the cultural sector do not understand what wide-ranging expertise is in museums and the range of work which they carry out. Don't be shy in suggesting that your change journey can be useful for others, as the human elements of change remain a constant challenge, whatever your sector.

See also:

29   Don't be afraid to report problems or 'failure'
39   Communicating change, internally and externally

Notes

1 R.R. Janes, *Museums and the paradox of change: A case study in urgent adaptation* (third edition, Routledge 2013), p. 101.
2 R.R. Janes, *Museums and the paradox of change: A case study in urgent adaptation* (third edition, Routledge 2013), p. 100.
3 R. Moilliet, 'How can evaluation and reflection become a useful part of everyday work?', in M. Miller, R. Moilliet and E. Daly (eds.), *Circuit – Test, Risk, Change: Young people, youth organisations and galleries working together* (Tate and Paul Hamlyn Foundation 2019), p. 427.
4 R.R. Janes, *Museums and the paradox of change: A case study in urgent adaptation* (third edition, Routledge 2013), p. 100.
5 R.R. Janes, *Museums and the paradox of change: A case study in urgent adaptation* (third edition, Routledge 2013), p. 294.
6 See H. Kemp-Welch, 'A digital democracy: The role of the *Circuit* website', in M. Miller, R. Moilliet and E. Daly (eds.), *Circuit – Test, Risk, Change: Young people, youth organisations and galleries working together* (Tate and Paul Hamlyn Foundation 2019), p. 496–501.
7 The Chatham House Rule was created in 1927 at the UK Royal Institute of International Affairs, based at Chatham House, London. The rule was most recently refined in 2002 and reads: 'When a meeting, or part thereof, is held under the Chatham House Rule, participants are free to use the information received, but neither the identity nor the affiliation of the speaker(s), nor that of any other participant, may be revealed'.
8 ofbyforall.org.

APPENDIX A

Resources to help you

This list focuses on ten practical web-based resources on change in museums and galleries, including three from outside the museum sector. They provide practical advice and case studies, and many include videos and self-assessment tools that are ideal for stimulating a discussion about change among staff, governing bodies and management teams.

ourmuseum.org.uk

Over 200 multi-media resources on organisational change and embedding community participation, with practical insights and case studies. You can either explore the pre-set categories or search for keywords, e.g. entering 'change process' into the search bar brings up numerous videos and other resources on how to achieve successful change.

circuit.tate.org.uk

Archive website of a national UK programme connecting young people and galleries. Includes research, articles and reports on supporting organisational change.

aim-museums.co.uk

From the Association of Independent Museums: Success Guides, covering all aspects of managing museums, especially strong on governance and developing boards; and the AIM Hallmarks, which identify characteristics that help museums and heritage organisations to adapt and thrive, with case studies.

happymuseumproject.org
Planning and review tools for organisational change (mostly based on workshop approaches), videos and case studies from the Happy Museum Project, which is concerned with how museums can become more sustainable and resilient.

Power to the People
Available on the Museums Association website, museumsassociation.org. A self-assessment framework designed to help museums improve their participatory practice and community engagement. Provides benchmarks of best practice across all aspects of museum work and is a useful tool for tracking organisational change.

museumtwo.blogspot.com
Internationally popular blog started in 2006 by Nina Simon, covering community engagement, change and the future of museums.

ofbyforall.org
Includes a self-assessment tool to check how your museum rates in being 'of, by and for' your community, and other toolkits and resources to help create and support change.

ted.com/talks/simon_sinek_how_great_leaders_inspire_action
Simon Sinek on inspirational leadership and finding your 'Why?' – why your museum exists and what it exists to do.

theoryofchange.org
The website of the Center for Theory of Change provides resources such as webinars, publications and technical assistance on the Theory of Change process.

changeleadersnetwork.com
A worldwide network of change leaders, including free articles and webinars on all aspects of organisational change.

APPENDIX B

Useful publications

This list focuses on publications which give at least some element of practical guidance about the process of change for those involved. It is not an exhaustive bibliography of publications about change in museums, many of which are theoretical, historical or philosophical and largely aimed at museum academics, or descriptions of innovative short-term projects or stirring calls to activism which might lead to change. The shortness of the list demonstrates how little has been published on this topic that is genuinely useful to practitioners needing to address the challenges and problems of change.

G. Anderson (ed.), *Reinventing the museum: The evolving conversation on the paradigm shift* (second edition, AltaMira Press 2012).

P. Bienkowski, *No longer us and them: How to change into a participatory museum and gallery – Learning from the Our Museum programme* (Paul Hamlyn Foundation 2016).

P. Bienkowski, 'Why change fails (and what YOU can do about it)', *Journal of Education in Museums* 37 (2017), pp. 13–21.

P. Bienkowski, *Our Museum: What happened next? A review and further learning two years on* (Paul Hamlyn Foundation 2018).

G. Black, *Museums and the challenge of change: Old institutions in a new world* (Routledge 2021).

A. Chynoweth, B. Lynch, K. Peterson and S. Smed (eds.), *Museums and social change: Challenging the unhelpful museum* (Routledge 2020).

R. Hewison, J. Holden and S. Jones, *All together: A creative approach to organisational change* (Demos 2010).

P. Holman, T. Devane and S. Cady (eds.), *The change handbook: The definitive resource on today's best methods for engaging whole systems* (second edition, Berrett-Koeher Publishers Inc. 2007).

R.R. Janes, *Museums and the paradox of change: A case study in urgent adaptation* (third edition, Routledge 2013).

S. Lee and K. Gean, *The Engagement Revolution: A study of strategic organizational transformation in 10 California arts nonprofits* (James Irvine Foundation 2017).

B. Lynch, *Whose cake is it anyway? A collaborative investigation into engagement and participation in 12 museums and galleries in the UK* (Paul Hamlyn Foundation 2011).

M. Miller, R. Moilliett and N. Jones, *Circuit – Test, Risk, Change* (Tate and Paul Hamlyn Foundation 2017).

M. Miller, R. Moilliet and E. Daly (eds.), *Circuit – Test, Risk, Change: Young people, youth organisations and galleries working together* (Tate and Paul Hamlyn Foundation 2019).

N. Morse and M. McCann, *Becoming a change-maker in museums: Experiences, opportunities and challenges: Reflections on the Museums Association's Transformers Workforce Development Initiative* (University of Leicester 2019).

Museums Association, *Power and privilege in the 21st century museum: Tactics for change from the Museums Association Transformers programme* (Museums Association 2019).

R. Sandell and R.R. Janes (eds.), *Museum management and marketing* (Routledge 2007).

N. Simon, *The participatory museum* (Museum 2.0 2010).

N. Simon, *The art of relevance* (Museum 2.0 2016).

R. Smith, D. King, R. Sidhu and D. Skelsey (eds.), *The effective change manager's handbook* (Kogan Page 2015).

INDEX

Note: Page numbers in *italics* indicate figures and page numbers in **bold** indicate tables.